Marjoe Gortner as Teddy, the psychotic Vietnam vet out to make life hell for the inhabitants of a small New Mexico diner in *When You Comin' Back, Red Ryder* (1979).

The Films of Marjoe Gortner

By John Harrison

Wildcat! The Films of Marjoe Gortner
Copyright © 2020 John Harrison. All Rights Reserved.

No part of this book may be reproduced in any form or by any means, electronic, mechanical, digital, photocopying or recording, except for inclusion in a review, without permission in writing from the publisher.

This book is an independent work of research and commentary and is not sponsored, authorized or endorsed by, or otherwise affiliated with, Marjoe Gortner, nor any of the filmmakers, performers, writers and studios discussed in this work. All uses of the name, image and likeness of Marjoe Gortner and all other individuals, and all copyrights and trademarks referenced in this book, are for editorial purposes only and are pursuant to the Fair Use Doctrine.

The views and opinions of individuals quoted in this book do not necessarily reflect those of the author.

The promotional photos and publicity materials reproduced herein are from the author's private collection (unless otherwise noted), and are Copyrighted by their respective owners. These images date from the original release of the films and were released to media outlets for publicity purposes. Any corrections will be noted in future editions.

Published in the USA by:
BearManor Media
1317 Edgewater Dr #110
Orlando, FL 32804
www.bearmanormedia.com

Printed in the United States of America

ISBN   978-1-62933-500-1 (paperback)
         978-1-62933-501-8 (hardback)

Book and cover design by Darlene Swanson • www.van-garde.com
Cover illustration by Pete Wallbank • www.petewallbankart.com

Contents

	Introduction.	xi
Chapter One	Giving The Devil Two Black Eyes: A Marjoe Gortner Primer	1
Chapter Two	Marjoe: The Documentary	19
Chapter Three	The Holy Hustler Hits Hollywood: The Marjoe Gortner Filmography	33
Chapter Four	Marjoe on the Groove Tube: Television Appearances	165
Chapter Five	Marjoe on Wax: Soundtracks & Recordings	205
Chapter Six	Marjoe: The Enduring Enigma	209
Appendix 1:	Bibliography	213
	Afterword	223
	About the Author	227
	Thank You	229
	Index	231

Dedicated To:

Marjoe & Marneen

*"My name is Marjoe Gortner,
I'm only four years old.
I'm coming to your town,
to shoot the Devil down.
So come and go with me,
and surely you will see.
Me preach the old-time gospel,
and have a jubilee."*

Introduction

"When this man gets up, be prepared to face the most powerful, emotional experience of your life."
—Poster tagline for *When You Comin' Back, Red Ryder.*

1968. A GRIMY roadside diner, somewhere in the middle of the bleak, hot New Mexico desert. A muscular young man, with tanned skin, curly dirty blonde locks and intense, intimidating eyes, prowls the interior of the greasy diner like a pent–up wild animal that is ready to pounce at any given moment. A small group of people are unfortunate enough to find themselves inside the diner at the same time: the timid waitress; the bored night shift worker; the elderly and crippled owner of the petrol station and motel next door, and an upper–middle–class couple passing through on their way to New Orleans. They all huddle in fear, terrified of the stranger's next move. Exhausted from the psychological wringer which he has already put them through, they sit nervously in wait for the inevitable moment when the torment will turn from emotional to physical. The man's girlfriend, a pretty young flower child, tensely watches over the scene and wonders which side she should be on.

Released in 1979, I first saw *When You Comin' Back, Red Ryder* when I stumbled across it during a rare late-night television screening in 1988, and though it was an eye–opener in terms of his talent and performance, it certainly wasn't my first exposure to Marjoe Gortner. I had snuck off into the city to see him in Bert I. Gordon's *The Food of the Gods* (1976) many years earlier, and I always recognized and enjoyed seeing his face whenever it popped up in other films and on television shows. He had a unique look and a screen presence that made him instantly identifiable and memorable.

But for all the enjoyment I was getting out of watching Marjoe Gortner on screen, for years I was completely unaware that I was only getting half of the story. It wasn't until the early nineties that I discovered the other side of Marjoe and finally began to realize that there was so much more to the man than his cinematic charisma and eclectic range of movie and television roles. I was reading a used hardcover copy of the excellent Beatles biography *The Love You Make*, written by Peter Brown and Steven Gaines and first published in 1983 by Macmillan. While going over the author bios on the inside dust jacket flap, I noticed that Gaines was credited as, amongst other things, "the author of *Marjoe*, the biography of evangelist Marjoe Gortner." Huh? The same Marjoe Gortner whose charismatic onscreen performances I had been enjoying for the past 15 years? In those days, easy access to the world wide web and databases like IMDB were still a few years away, so it wasn't as easy as it is today to do a quick Google search and verify some information, but surely there could not be two people in the world with such a unique name? And Marjoe's performance in *When You Comin' Back, Red Ryder* certainly had the intensity and maniacal edge of a dark pop evangelist. The plot thickened, and my curiosity grew. I soon found confirmation, if I needed any, in the pages of Danny Peary's *Cult Movie Stars* (1991, Fireside/Simon & Schuster), a large, thick paperback that I had found sitting on the shelves of Melbourne's (sadly now–gone) Moviola, a wonderful store that specialized in

Introduction

film books and memorabilia. I plunked down the cash for *Cult Movie Stars* on the spot, since I was already something of a fan of the author's work, having admired his writing in his *Cult Movies* series of books (the first of which contained a terrific essay of Tobe Hooper's *The Texas Chainsaw Massacre* that exerted a huge influence on myself, both as a film fan and when I started to explore my own interest in film journalism and criticism). An offshoot of sorts of his *Cult Movies* books, *Cult Movie Stars* provided an A–Z encyclopedia of over 750 actors and actresses that had established some level of cult following amongst certain devotees. When I saw that Marjoe had an entry in there, it was a surprise but also a welcome confirmation that I clearly wasn't the only one out there who had some degree of fascination with, and appreciation of, Marjoe Gortner and his work. Peary's entry on Marjoe was brief, but at least it was accompanied by a nice black & white photo of him (a still with co-star Candy Clark from *Red Ryder*), and it confirmed the actor's past career as *"a showy itinerant child evangelist."*

Marjoe's entry in *Cult Movie Stars* also made mention of an Oscar-winning 1972 documentary called—appropriately enough—*Marjoe*, which instantly shot to the top of my must-see list. There was still a large number of grey-area and underground (i.e., bootleg) video trading companies around at that time, mostly comprising of one person with a large video collection and two VCRs hooked-up in order to run off dubs to sell or trade amongst other collectors. After scanning through a number of advertisements in an issue of *Psychotronic Video* magazine, I came in touch with a dealer in the US who was offering a copy of *Marjoe* on VHS, and a few weeks after sending off my international money order for US $37.00 ($25.00 for the movie and the rest for air postage) a plain VHS tape with 'Marjoe' scrawled across the label in black marker turned up in the mail. At the time my VCR was not multi-format so I couldn't even play the NTSC tape on my machine, but I spent pretty much every afternoon for the next week at one of the audio–visual booths at Swinburne University, compulsively watching that grainy, fifth generation (at least) VHS tape on one of their multi–format machines and dutifully studying Marjoe Gortner's astonishing transition from child to man.

Publicity portrait of Marjoe Gortner taken in July 1973, not long after he had abandoned evangelism in favor of a career as an actor and entertainer.

Introduction

Once you become aware of Marjoe's childhood and background, it's almost impossible to watch him on film without thoughts of his energetic and charismatic sermons swimming around in your head. Maybe it's unfair to connect the two, after all Marjoe—like any other actor—deserves to be accepted and evaluated on his talents in that field alone. Yet Marjoe's case is distinctively unique, and it's clear from watching him onscreen (particularly in a film like *Red Ryder*) that he draws so deeply from his past, or at least what he has learned from it, to compose his performances and fictional characters, which is one of the aspects to Marjoe that make him so absorbing to watch and study.

Wildcat! is not intended to be a definitive or in-depth biography of Marjoe Gortner himself. Marjoe's early years were covered quite well in Gaines' *Marjoe* book as well as the documentary. What I have set out to do with this book is to primarily celebrate the screen career of this unique individual, and examine Marjoe's filmography and the way in which each role fits into Gortner's overall oeuvre.

If you are already an established admirer of Marjoe's work, I hope this book opens your eyes a little bit wider. Likewise, if you are just starting to explore the wonderful world of Marjoe Gortner, let *Wildcat!* be your suitably informative and entertaining tour guide.

CHAPTER ONE

Giving The Devil Two Black Eyes: A Marjoe Gortner Primer

HIS NAME BEING an amalgam of the biblical names Mary and Joseph, Marjoe Gortner was born Hugh Marjoe Ross Gortner in Long Beach, California on January 14, 1944. Born into a family with a long line of evangelical heritage, it was perhaps no surprise that Marjoe was groomed as a preacher from an early age. His father Vernon Gortner, along with his grandfather Narver and great grandfather Ross, were all ordained ministers. Ross Gortner tragically died from a serious malaria outbreak while on a preaching mission to Liberia, while Narver, originally a Methodist minister, turned to the Pentecostal church after experiencing an episode of speaking in tongues during a prayer camp held in the forests of Cozadero, California. Growing up within this environment, there was no doubt that young Vernon Gortner would follow in their footsteps. He was ordained at twenty and quickly went on to form his own ministry, the Lighthouse Tabernacle in Brooklyn.

While Vernon married in 1922 and spent nearly two decades enjoying the perceived life of a happily married and successful minister, his personal and professional lives both took a huge unexpected turn in 1940, when he booked the Canadian Sisters to appear at his church. The Canadian Sisters were not siblings at all, but rather two young women, Marge McMillan and Leone Blonde, who were brought together for purely professional reasons, to form an attractive pair of travelling evangelists who would please the eye while delivering dynamic sermons across North America. The adopted daughter of Reverend H. Stuart McMillan, Marge McMillan was well aware of the persuasive art of showmanship, and how much it could increase revenue, and Vernon, already realizing he would need to keep his act fresh to sustain its earnings, was completely intoxicated and won over by the tall, striking blonde. By the time their two-week booking had finished, Vernon's marriage and his ministry had virtually collapsed, and the Canadian Sisters disbanded, as Vernon and Marge (twelve years his junior) quickly fell in love and became inseparable. The pair moved to Las Vegas and were married as soon as Vernon's divorce was finalized, though the separation proved to be a crippling one financially, as he was ordered by the courts to make enormous alimony payments to his ex-wife for her upkeep and the livelihood of their four children, and his excommunication from his church in the wake of the scandal meant he was not able to bring in the sort of money he was previously.

Broke and desperate, Vernon and Marge relocated to a rental house in Long Beach, California, where Vernon pondered how he could make his now miserable wife happy again. A new Pentecostal church he established in the area quickly failed and Vernon had to resort to taking a job selling liniments and spices for the Minnesota-based J.R. Watkins Company. Vernon's preaching background obviously helped make him a good salesman, as his work with the Watkins Company proved so successful that he soon opened up his own store in Long Beach to distribute their products, with Marge helping behind the counter and another lady, Flo Laverne, hired to do the bookkeeping. The business grew big enough for Vernon and Marge to buy an oceanfront property and afford the services of a maid named Nadine, though Marge continued to be disappointed in what her life had become, and refused to return to the shop after a confrontation with an armed robber.

Marge's depression grew worse when she discovered she had fallen pregnant in May of 1943. A child, along with the proliferation of new evangelists who had taken to the road, meant there was little chance she would recapture the glory of her past. But when little Marjoe finally made his appearance (after a fifty-hour labor that eventually required a Caesarean to successfully deliver the baby), Marge was quick to declare him as a gift from God, and her ticket to a better life. She later claimed little Marjoe learned to say words like "glory" and "hallelujah" long before he could say "mama" and "papa", and kept him apart from other small children while she introduced him to the local preachers and enrolled him in classes to learn the accordion and baton-twirling, skills that would help give the child a further edge of showmanship.

While Marjoe welcomed the arrival of a younger brother, Vernoe, on June 19, 1946, the attention of his parents—in particular, Marge—was still fully on him. With his third birthday approaching, Marjoe made his first public appearance, marching down Hollywood Boulevard in the annual Christmas parade, twirling his rhinestone-covered baton while dressed in a white satin outfit. Within a year, after having his curly locks dyed blonde and spending hours upon hours memorizing lines and scriptures, Marge was ready to present her 'miracle child' to the world. The Gortners rented Symphony Hall in Los Angeles for a gospel meeting, ensuring they invited plenty of local press to the occasion. A small wooden pulpit, measuring twenty-six inches in height, was specially built for the event, at which Marjoe, flashbulbs going off in his face, recited his well-rehearsed six–minute speech that Jesus had come to visit him in his sleep, telling the boy that it was his job to help spread the Holy Word. Though the event resulted in a few small photos and articles making the newspapers in L.A. and New York, it didn't have the traction which Vernon and Marge had hoped, nor did it lead to any financially lucrative offers.

Young Marjoe Gortner, dressed in his white suit with black bow tie and red carnation, delivering his well-rehearsed sermon of fire and brimstone for the newsreel cameras.

The story was in danger of being quickly forgotten about, until a seasoned journalist named Louis P. Wolfe spotted it and decided there could be some traction and further public interest in young Marjoe and his unique talents. It was Wolfe who suggested to the Gortners that Marjoe's story would be even more sensational, and subsequently, more lucrative, if he were to become an ordained minister. At the time, there was no legal minimum age for ordination in California, and on Halloween, October 31, 1948, four-year-old Marjoe Gortner, dressed in a velvet and satin suit, was ordained by Essie Binkley West, a local minister who became known as the "Angel of Skid Row" due to her work with the local homeless and down-and-out at the Sunshine Mission. Again, while the stunt garnered some scattered newspaper headlines and stories, and led to Marjoe speaking at a few churches and meetings, it didn't lead to the kind of exposure that the Gortners, Marge in particular, were hoping for. But the next publicity gimmick which Wolfe and the Gortners dreamt up together would finally do the trick and bring Marjoe to the attention of households all across America.

Now that he was an ordained minister, Wolfe suggested that Marjoe should do what ministers are best at and preside over a marriage. Once again, there was no law at the time placing an age restriction on ministers performing a wedding ceremony, and although Essie West was vehemently against the idea, the Gortners quickly located Virginia West (no relation to Essie), who owned a marriage chapel in Long Beach, and soon found a couple of young lovebirds who were willing to take part in the unusual ceremony. Twenty-three-year-old Raymond Miller was a merchant seaman who had met Alma Brown, twenty-one, only two weeks earlier and the pair were keen to tie the knot before Miller was shipped off to sea again. Louis Wolfe found the pair lining up at the Long beach marriage bureau and quickly made an arrangement for them to be married in a gimmick (but legal) ceremony by a four-year-old kid.

The marriage ceremony took place at the Normandy Chapel on January 4, 1949. Wearing a black velvet suit with white cowboy boots, a nervous Marjoe raced through the ceremony while cameras clicked and the Paramount newsreel camera whirred, finishing it off with a triumphant cry of "Raymond, kiss ya bride!" Though Virginia West was furious with the Gortners for using her chapel for what she ultimately decided was a cheap publicity stunt that showed her and her establishment in a bad light, the ceremony had its intended effect and landed Marje and Vernon the nationwide publicity they craved. Virginia West was not the only one horrified by the event, with clergymen everywhere expressing concerns about a dangerous precedent being set, and raising doubts about the legality of the whole thing. Though the Gortners had made sure Marjoe was legally entitled to perform the marriage ceremony, they had clearly taken advantage of the law, and the following year a new law was introduced at a meeting of the California state legislature, which set twenty–one as the minimum age for both ordination and for performing a wedding ceremony.

The Marjoe Gortner roadshow had begun.

The Gortners spent the next decade on the road, a travelling religious roadshow which bordered on carnival freakshow. Fabricating a story (prepared by his parents, of course) that he had received a vision from God while taking a bath one evening, Marjoe was trotted out and put on display at churches and revival tents for the God–fearing public to marvel over and throw money at. Whenever Marjoe the miracle child tried to go against his parents' wishes or showed any signs on insubordination towards them, they responded by holding his head under water until he was gasping for air (they did not resort to beating him as they did not want to leave any tell–tale marks or bruises over his body).

Newspaper advertisement from the January 7, 1950, edition of *The Tampa Tribune*, promoting Marjoe's appearances at the Municipal Auditorium the following day.

So popular did the Marjoe show become that it created a lucrative mini–industry for the Gortners. A book entitled *Marjoe: A Modern Miracle* was put together in 1948 and reprinted several times over the following few years. This was followed in November 1950 by the first issue of *Twilight Tidings*, a newsletter that could be subscribed to for a dollar a year. Edited and put together by Flo Laverne, *Twilight Tidings* consisted of a handful of pages that reprinted the texts of Marjoe's sermons and, of course, pleas for donations to pay for the Gortners' travels and equipment (most notably, their revival tent which they claimed cost over fourteen thousand dollars). Essentially, *Twilight Tidings* was a way for the Gortners to both build a database of mailing addresses (and potential donators) as well as a tool to sell Marjoe-related merchandise, including a record album featuring some of his more memorable and dynamic sermons (see the "Recordings" chapter of this book for further information on Marjoe's recording career).

Knowing full well that the majority of Marjoe's fame and appeal was in the fact that he was so young, the Gortners realized they would have to make their fortune from him in a hurry, before he outgrew his cuteness and novelty status. Vernon, Marge, Marjoe and Vernoe, accompanied by their two chihuahuas Bambi and Blueboe, criss-crossed the United States in their Buick "Woodie" station wagon, initially staying in local hotels wherever Marjoe performed but later investing in a large trailer to tow around and live in. Vernon would take care of the promotion as soon as the travelling show hit a new town, contacting the local newspapers and taking out advertisements in the entertainment pages (he refused to advertise in any religious supplements as he claimed he would reach more sinners willing to pay for repentance via the entertainment section).

To keep crowds coming back during multi-night stays or return visits to local towns, theme nights were often organized, where Marjoe would perform magic tricks or dress-up as a shepherd (complete with staff and stuffed lamb). Western nights were a popular theme, both with the crowds and Marjoe himself, who loved western movies and television shows even though his parents refused to let him watch anything that suggested violence or involved guns. So strong was the Gortners' stance on the issue that they even refused an invitation from western legend Roy Rogers for Marjoe to appear on his enormously popular television show. There was also Family Night, in which the largest family in attendance would win a prize, usually an original piece of religious art that would be painted on the spot by Forrest Potter, an artist who started working for the Gortners as a volunteer driver and tent-pitcher before graduating to displaying and selling his art at the shows.

Potter was not the only "gospel groupie" that the Gortner roadshow attracted. People with too much time on their hands and too much money in their pockets would often follow the Gortners from town to town, dishing out donations and being a regular face for a few weeks or months at a time and then disappearing back into the heartland. One dubious gentleman even made cash donations in return for various items of little Marjoe's clothing, which he would then describe in disturbing detail how he was displaying the memorabilia in his home. Most parents would have been alarmed or repulsed by such a pastime, but to the Gortners the donations made everything acceptable and in the name of good, wholesome religious values.

By 1952 the Gortner roadshow had managed to infiltrate virtually all areas of the United States (one exception being New England, where evangelism was looked down upon). Now eight-years-old, little Marjoe was going through big changes, both physically and emotionally. Since first hitting the preaching circuit, he had grown tall and gangly and his childish cuteness was starting to dissipate. In addition, the novelty was starting to wear off and the local publicity he attracted whenever he hit town was not as prominent as it once was. A shorter haircut exposed Marjoe's rather prominent and protruding ears which further diminished his initial cutesy appeal. Marge resorted to gluing his ears back whenever Marjoe was about to make a public appearance or was booked for a photo session, before eventually taking him to Cincinnati to have them permanently pinned back by a plastic surgeon.

Naturally, as time went on and the Gortners hit the same towns time after time, and with Marjoe starting to grow, the financial coffers were not filling up as high or as regularly as they used to. In desperation, Marge decided to incorporate faith healing into Marjoe's act, and she took the boy to watch and study the faith healing methods of Jesse, Andrew and Frank Kirkwood, three famous brothers from Baton Rouge who each ran their own travelling evangelical and faith healing shows. While the addition of faith healing to Marjoe's shows provided a temporary boost in attendance and donations, by the mid–fifties the once–prosperous roadshow was well and truly on its last legs, and with Vernoe and adopted younger sister Starloe (born 1950) both failing to follow in Marjoe's footsteps, tensions between Vernon and Marge became more and more strained as their financial situation became more and more precarious. Though Vernon would always blame the high expenses of keeping the show on the road whenever he was asked why there was little money in the bank, Marge had her doubts and began to grow ever more suspicious about her husband and where all the money was really going.

While 1956 may have been a bad one for the Gortners' finances, it was a memorable one for Marjoe, as he lost his virginity at age twelve to the sixteen–year–old daughter of the local pastor in Danville, Virginia. Not long after, as Marjoe was preparing for a revival meeting in Charlotte, North Carolina, Marge returned to their hotel room to collect Vernon, only to find an empty room with a five–dollar bill and a note sitting on top of the dressing table. Vernon had left and was heading for California, absconding with the life savings and leaving Marge, the two boys and Starloe broke and fending for themselves. By the dawn of the sixties, Marjoe's glory days as a child evangelist were fading into history, and to distance himself from what he once was, he began to adapt his middle name Ross as he landed a series of odd jobs, including working as a cook at a truck stop diner near Santa Cruz which Marge had established with the help of a new man she had begun dating. While Marjoe/Ross may have felt a bit out of place in a greasy chef's hat and apron, he thrived in the old world carnie atmosphere that permeated the neon-lit boardwalk of Santa Cruz, and he soon found his old talents keeping himself in good stead when local huckster Herbert Cunningham offered him a job running a game in which punters plunked down a dime to bet on a race between plastic toy horses.

Still hiding behind the name Ross, Marjoe's boardwalk style was so effective it not only allowed him to quit his night job at his mom's diner, but also provided him with the perfect opportunity to meet an abundance of young women just as the age of sexual liberation was starting to dawn. With his earnings, Ross bought himself a Volkswagen VW bug to help him explore both his sexuality as well as his independence. The cramped backseat of the VW was likely where Ross got Ann, his first real girlfriend whom he had met on the boardwalk, pregnant. Though Marge implored the couple to have an abortion, and even encouraged her son to simply disappear and head back east, Ross refused to shirk his responsibilities, and the young couple headed for the wedding chapels of Reno, Nevada, after which they settled into a small rented apartment in Santa Cruz.

Ann Gortner gave birth to a girl, whom they named Gigi, on March 2, 1961. By this point Ross had taken on a role as a trainee manager with the Standard Oil Company, a position that was much more lucrative that working the boardwalk or his mother's diner, but one which required the young parents to relocate to the rather isolated small town of King City (population at the time: 2,000). Ross felt a deep boredom with his life and marriage, compounded when he became housebound and confined to a lower body cast after damaging one of the lumbar discs in his back. Unable to work and with the bills mounting, Ross sought financial help from both of his parents but was turned down. Disillusioned and bored, Ross buried himself in books and practicing the organ, which he had rented from a local music store.

Once his back had healed and the cast removed, Ross headed for Los Angeles to look for a new job that would enable him to escape the banality and boredom of King City, and his stifling home life with Ann. He soon found a job as a shoe salesman for the Innes Shoe Store chain, hardly his dream profession but one which at least allowed him to relocate to L.A. and hopefully put a bit of excitement back into his marriage to Ann. Though the work was mind-numbing and monotonous, Marjoe—still using the name Ross—proved a natural at selling shoes, just as he had proved successful on the Santa Cruz boardwalk. He soon found himself working at the Innes' prestigious Beverly Hills store, wearing designer suits and having his hair cut by Jay Sebring, the famous hairdresser to the stars whose life would be tragically cut short by disciples of crazed cult leader Charles Manson in August of 1969.

It was while working at the shoe store that Ross, thanks to a wholesale shoe salesman that he dealt with, first tried marijuana. Though only twenty, he had told everyone he worked with that he was twenty-five, feeling it would help people take him more seriously if they thought he was older and more mature. Ross still felt bored and stifled in his marriage, but he and Ann managed to inject a bit of excitement into their lives by enjoying the burgeoning music and dance clubs that were starting to open up along Sunset Strip, such as the Peppermint West (the L.A. branch of the New York's famed Peppermint Lounge) and the Surf Club, where many of the waitresses moonlighted as hookers and where Ross soon found some work as a part-time pimp, acting as a middle-man to help bashful patrons connect with the waitress of their liking. With the blessings of her older husband, Ross himself also hooked-up at the Surf Club with a lady in her forties named Joanne, and the pair would spend afternoons at the tennis court and evenings at a motel room for the following year, until both it and Ross's marriage to Ann ended at around the same time. While Ann moved into an apartment with their daughter, Ross remained living in the house, filling his time with a "hobby" rock band called the Grim Reapers which he had put together. The lead guitarist for the Grim Reapers, a part-time drug dealer named Steve Klein, moved in with Ross and quickly turned him onto LSD, the psychedelic drug that was becoming one of the focal points of the counterculture movement that was now emerging and which Ross had been reading about and watching on the news with much interest. While Ross had continued to smoke pot after being introduced to it, it was his experimentation with LSD which really helped him to crystalize his thoughts and perception, and he began dropping acid before heading into the shoe store, in order to better "read" his customers and co-workers. Unfortunately, the continual stream of customers who turned up to Ross' house in order to score dope from Steve Klein quickly turned the place into a crazy and chaotic crash pad, with clothes, furniture and electric goods mysteriously disappearing without trace.

It wasn't until he met Stephanie Hollander, a twenty-four-year-old who moved from New York to Los Angeles in 1967 in search of her own slice of the peace and love movement, that Ross began to look back upon his child evangelist days. The pair first met at the shoe store, where Ross took a chance on Stephanie by going against store policy and cashing a third–party check, issued by a restaurant that the girl had just been fired from. Though cautious at first, Stephanie's attitude towards Ross began to relax when she saw him out of his business clothes for the first time. With his hair loose instead of slicked back and old jeans replacing his suit pants, he looked more in line with the young counterculture type that she has come to L.A. to meet. For their first date together, Ross took Stephanie to a club where his band The Grim Reapers were performing that night. When the group hit the stage and launched into a cacophony of out–of–synch noise, Stephanie began to think that Ross' future did not belong in the music industry. However, once Ross moved away from his electric organ and stood at the microphone to sing, the whole energy and ambience in the club seemed to change. Ross' command of the microphone, the confidence he exuded and the complete control he took of the audience revealed something very special and unexpected to Stephanie, and they were soon living together and enjoying road trips up and down the California coast, sleeping in tents and attending the famous Monterey Pop Festival, a three–day event held between June 16—18 of 1967, at which such acts as the Jefferson Airplane, The Who, Otis Redding, the Jimi Hendrix Experience, the Mamas & the Papas and Indian sitar guru Ravi Shankar performed. The day before the Monterey event started, Ross and Stephanie were treated to something of a private performance by Shankar, when the pair stumbled across him in a field playing for a small crowd. Shankar of course would exert a huge influence on the Beatles, in particular lead guitarist George Harrison, during their *Revolver* and *Sgt. Pepper's Lonely Hearts Club Band* period of the mid–sixties.

It was after the pair attended a Students for Democracy meeting at UCLA, where Ross took the microphone and mesmerized the audience the same way he had at the Grim Reapers gig, that Stephanie began to get a true insight into his past life and infamy. Stephanie was no doubt drop-jawed and incredulous as her partner began to detail his former life as Marjoe Gortner, the world's youngest ordained minister whose career behind the pulpit was washed-up before he reached puberty. When Marjoe informed Stephanie that his father was holding on to a huge scrapbook featuring all his old newspaper clippings, she insisted that he call Vernon and request that he send the scrapbook to them so she could see it for herself. It was a conversation and a phone call that would change their lives and lead to the public re-emergence of Marjoe Gortner.

****

The second coming of Marjoe was not launched without its moments of difficulty and tension. Opening up about his past to Stephanie also meant opening up old wounds and exposing her to truths that Marjoe had been hiding from her. Stephanie was somewhat shocked to discover that not only had Marjoe previously been married and had a young daughter, but Ann was still technically his wife since they did not pursue divorce proceedings after separating. Getting hold of all of Marjoe's clippings, old pulpit and other memorabilia meant reconnecting with his parents and introducing Stephanie to their world. En route to Oakland to collect his memorabilia from his father, Marjoe and Stephanie decided to stop by Ann's house to bring Ginny along on their road trip. By the time they reached Vernon's house the pair were stoned and exhausted, and they had to pretend to be married in order to be welcomed into the father's home. After polite introductions, Marjoe sent Stephanie and Ginny off into Berkley for a few hours while he caught up with Vernon and gathered up his old possessions. When the two girls returned later in the day, there was obvious tension hanging in the air between father and son, and Marjoe advised they would not be staying overnight as originally planned. Problems had arisen between Marjoe and Vernon over money—Vernon was trying to get money out of Marjoe in exchange for his scrapbooks and memorabilia, while Marjoe had been questioning his father over where all the money went that he had earned for the family during his childhood. With neither party ending up satisfied, Marjoe loaded up their vehicle (an old bus) with his belongings and the pair took off.

The final alignment of all the elements necessary to get Marjoe back at the pulpit was an act of either divine interference or clumsy bad luck. Returning to work at the shoe store not long after his road trip with Stephanie, Marjoe fell down the flight of stairs leading to the basement stockroom, re-injuring his back along with his calves and buttocks. Once again laid-up at home recovering and worried about how he was going to make ends meet during the long recuperation process, Marjoe received a visit from Maxwell Van Rellin, a former World War I shipbuilder who now owned the house which Marjoe and Stephanie were renting. Van Rellin's father had been a minister, so when he saw Marjoe's collection of clippings that had been spread out on the bed, they began trading stories and Van Rellin, fascinated by Marjoe's past life, asked the former child evangelist if he had ever considered a comeback to the pulpit, using the hook of "The Return of the Miracle Child" to garner publicity and draw both the old faithful and new curiosity seekers in. Marjoe confessed that the idea had been bouncing around inside his head for some time, and Van Rellin was soon back with a large leather scrapbook which he presented to Marjoe in order for him to organize all of his clippings. Van Rellin's generosity continued once Marjoe had sufficiently healed enough for he and Stephanie to take a camping vacation on the piece of Palm Springs land which Van Rellin owned. The elderly landlord further surprised Marjoe when he presented him with a one-hundred-dollar check, travelling money to get he and Stephanie to Texas so they could hook up with Brother Lucas, an old acquaintance whose ministry had started over thirty years earlier during the Great Depression. Marjoe had contacted Brother Lucas out of the blue by telephone and, after announcing his intent to return to the gospel circuit, had received an invitation to perform at the ministry's next revival meeting in a week's time.

Rather than use the hundred dollars generously provided by Van Rellin for necessities like food and petrol, Marjoe instead took Stephanie to the local beauty parlor. Marjoe knew that any congregation would have to accept the couple as two of their own in order for them to be listened to and taken seriously (and of course, to give freely of donations). A long-haired hippy gal in San Antonio was not likely to be integrated very far, so Stephanie's hair was tied-up in a respectable bun and her jeans and shirt skirts put into storage, while Marjoe had his curly locks clipped short and neat and packed his suit and ties into a suitcase. The couple's two dogs, Thrupence and Briar, were unfortunate casualties of Marjoe's re-awakening. Animals were not likely to be welcomed at the motels they would be staying at, so Marjoe made the tough decision to give the dogs over to the owner of a ranch just outside of L.A.

Act Two of Marjoe's public life had begun...

CHAPTER TWO

Marjoe: The Documentary

As THE BORN–AGAIN Marjoe Gortner barnstormed his way across the American South, New York–born couple Sarah Kernochan and Howard Smith, partners in both life and creativity, were on the lookout for their next project when Gortner's name came into their sights. Marjoe, who by now was juggling his time between Los Angeles and New York and was trying to make inroads as an actor and musician, had reached out to Smith, at the time working as a columnist for the *Village Voice*, about the possibility of being profiled in the magazine, or on the radio talk show which Smith also hosted. Though Smith did have Marjoe on his radio show as a guest, it was mostly Kernochan who saw greater potential in the subject, not so much as a magazine article for the *Village Voice* but more as a feature documentary film. Neither Smith nor Kernochan had much filmmaking experience to that point, but the later, at the time only twenty–five and a decade younger than her partner, was already writing screenplays with the ambition to move towards film production. Striking up an agreement with Marjoe, Smith and Kernochan, along with their small crew of cinematographers and sound recordists, accompanied Gortner to revival meetings in Los Angeles, Anaheim, Detroit and Fort Worth, capturing the preacher and his audience in unflinching detail after being granted unrestricted access by the ministers holding the meetings in each city (who obviously had no idea of the true intentions of the filmmakers or the damning direction which the documentary would ultimately take).

Released by Cinema 5 Distributing, when *Marjoe* hit American cinemas on July 24, 1972 it provided a riveting and eye–opening experience for those who went along to see it, many no doubt expecting little more than an off–beat curio but emerging either saddened, angered or just plain astonished (often various measures of all three) by what they had witnessed. The documentary came along at an opportune time: the sixties had ended and the communal counterculture was giving way to the greed of the "Me" decade, and televangelism, though it had started infiltrating the medium in the early–fifties, was approaching new heights of exposure and controversy thanks to the immense popularity of broadcasts featuring evangelists like Jimmy Swaggart and the Bakers (Jim and Tammy Faye), many of whom would ultimately be exposed and come undone by greed or salacious scandal.

Marjoe opens with a vintage color newsreel clip of Marge introducing the little evangelist, intertwined with black & white photos and a voice–over of Marjoe reflecting on his childhood sermons before cutting to a present–day clip of an adult, energetic Marjoe popping up from behind what seems like an old brick barbeque, which is sitting on the grounds of his property, and launching into a jolly rendition of his signature introductory jingle:

"My name is Marjoe Gortner, I'm only four–years–old. I'm coming to your town. to shoot the Devil down. So come and go with me, and surely you will see, me preach the old–time gospel, and have a jubilee."

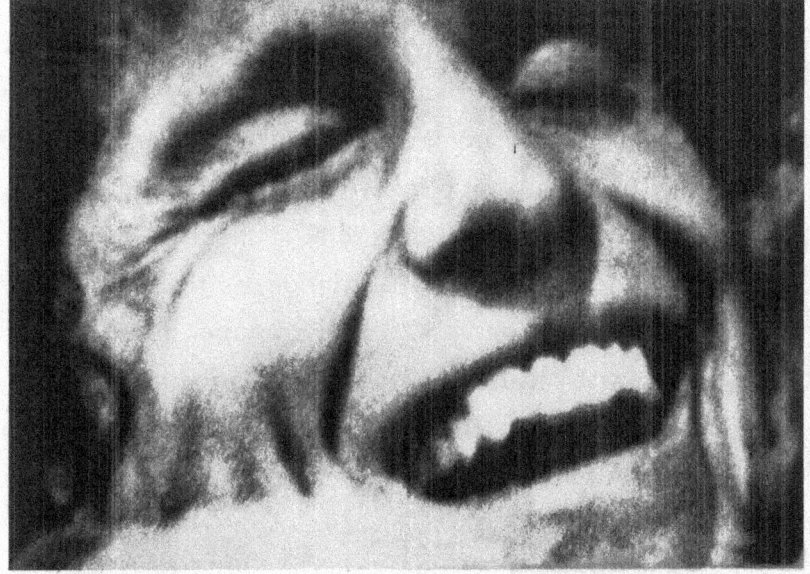

Low–tech but effective American poster design for *Marjoe*.

Having provided us with a crash–course in Marjoe 101 and introducing us to the man which the little boy became, *Marjoe* wastes no time in drawing us in with its cinéma verité style, as Marjoe holds court with the film crew in his small hotel room, instructing them on how they should conduct themselves when they are out filming him in the field and, in particular, when he is around other preachers and authority figures. Smoking and long hair on men seem to be particular no–no's according to Marjoe, the later not so much because it might scare or shock someone but more because a religious zealot might spot a male with long hair and automatically assume he is troubled and in need of saving. Fraternizing with young females ("revival groupies", as Marjoe describes them) is also strongly discouraged ("I never take a girl from the church, or in the church. I stick with airline stewardesses"). Marjoe then delivers a favorite passage from his sermons to help inspire the young (and clearly counterculture–oriented) filmmakers to get into the converted frame of mind:

"For seven years I was a heroin addict. A pill–popper, LSD tripper. High–ridin' and low–slidin'. Bustin' heads and droppin' reds. Kickin' in doors and bangin' whores. Settin' fires and slashin' tyres. But then I met a man who was hung-up on my hang–ups!"

Casually sitting on the floor in a pair of blue denim bell–bottoms and a purple tie–dyed singlet, Gortner comes across here as very soft–spoken, shy and somewhat nervous. He knows what a big deal all this is to him, to his future as well as to his reputation and the clear risks he is taking by choosing to open up about the secrets of his profession. There are big smiles and laughter, both from Marjoe and the film crew, but there is also a palpable tension within the room, with both sides feeling each other out and trying to form a trustworthy working bond and solidifying the shape which the documentary will take (though it already seems clear from this point that the film will be an exposé, as the filmmakers voice concern over arousing the suspicion of other preachers and followers).

"Are we going to film Marjoe's crucifixion when they find out about all of this?", asks one of the filmmakers, as talk turns to what may happen when those trusting the film crew enough to let them into their congregation discover the true motives behind the documentary.

"I'm hoping that they'll see that it's not necessary to look to some person to, like, jerk you off to get off, and put your belief in", Marjoe answers somewhat nervously before the film cuts to a revival meeting already in full swing, the flock of followers possessed by the music and held in a trance by the words of wisdom and faith, as Marjoe takes the microphone and begins to assume charge of the proceedings. Watching Marjoe return to his childhood vocation as an adult in his late–twenties is little short of mesmerizing. Sweat–drenched, tight–clothed and wild–eyed, Gortner struts before his congregation like a born–again Mick Jagger in prime *Gimme Shelter* form, the blood–red carpet beneath his feet giving an impression of him walking miraculously across flowing lava, or the fire and brimstone of Hell that he warns the congregation about. After whipping his audience into a frenzy and luring them into the palm of his hand with a repeated, exhausted plea of "Hallelujah! Thank You, Jesus!", Marjoe then whips out the "prayer cloths", ostensibly just cheap red–colored bandanas which Gortner now claims to be imbued with healing or faith–inducing powers, including the ability the cure people from drug addiction! And of course, one of these prayer cloths can be yours for a simple donation of the largest bill which you currently have on you. With worshippers falling to the floor in convulsions at the mere touch of one of Gortner's magic prayer cloths, the items start selling like holy hotcakes, forcing Marjoe's minders to start tearing them in half just to try and keep up with the demand.

While the sequences of Marjoe at the pulpit controlling his audience like a master puppeteer are riveting, it's the quieter and more intimate moments that prove to be the most revelatory, as Marjoe starts to lower his public façade and talk about the true nature of the business he is in. And business is exactly what he sees it as, noting that the most successful evangelists are the ones who run their churches as businessmen, "like Madison Avenue P. R. men." The power and importance of a good gimmick is also driven home by Marjoe, who reveals that one of his own favorite gimmicks was to apply a cross on his forehead in a special flesh-colored theatrical make-up before the show, then as the show proceeded and became more fervent and energetic, the sweat beading on his forehead would react with the make-up, turning it dark and making it appear as if the cross is miraculously materializing on his skin.

Sitting shirtless and cross-legged on a motel bed after a sermon, adrenalin still clearly pumping through him, Marjoe empties a big paper bag filled with bills from that evening's donations and proclaims that "Jesus is so good to me tonight", though as he starts counting out the bills and separating them into (mostly one and five-dollar) denominations he notes that the money bag "Sure isn't as heavy as it used to be, though. In the old days. Wow, it was really heavy then."

In moments filmed away from the revival tents and motels, Gortner reflects on love and relationships and the freedom of being able to live as himself during his non-preaching years, which he describes as a very transitional period in his life. A private outdoor lunch with a Texas minister and his wife is dominated by envious talk of a rival and his impressive mailing list of supporters that he sells copies of for a hefty fee. Other sequences of the documentary take place at a private party where pot fills the air and Marjoe, in loud western shirt, tries his best to fit in and look confident and cool but there are moments where you can sense an insecurity within him, as though he is not sure of how to act naturally in a social setting without having to be "Marjoe."

After earlier hearing Marjoe describe how his father up and left his family and lamenting the three–million–plus which he figures his parents earned off him during his child preaching days, an on-screen reunion with Vernon at a revival meeting is not as dramatic or tense as one might anticipate, the younger Gortner respectfully watching on and sharing a few chuckles as dad addresses the congregation and regales them with stories of his son's childhood and miraculous discovery of God.

The final moments of *Marjoe* feature Gortner relaxed and playful at home with his black Labrador and then–wife, an African–American woman named Agnes Benjamin who reveals that the first thing Marjoe did when they went out together was to bring her back to his apartment, where he spent the whole night showing her his scrapbook and playing his old preaching records. Benjamin, whom Marjoe had married in 1971 after separating from Stephanie, reacts with shock and disbelief when she is asked on camera if she believes Gortner is a conman (though she doesn't offer an actual reply), and observes that watching Marjoe deliver a sermon was akin to "watching a performance" by a stage actor, another person completely removed from who they really were offstage and behind closed doors.

Though *Marjoe* did not enjoy a long run in theatres (not an uncommon fate for documentaries, and the distributors were reluctant to screen the film below the Bible Belt), Smith and Kernochan's efforts were rewarded with positive reviews and ultimately an Academy Award for Best Documentary at the 45th Academy Awards held on March 27, 1973. Facing some stiff competition (most notably from Robert Hendrickson and Laurence Merrick's galvanizing *Manson*), when the co–directors walked to the podium of the Dorothy Chandler Pavilion in Los Angeles to collect their gold statuettes, one name was noticeably missing from their acceptance speech. Marjoe Gortner, the man whose life was at the very center of the film, did not rate a single mention from either Smith or Kernochan. Marjoe, it seems, had made something of a nuisance of himself during the post-production of the documentary, resulting in Kernochan and Smith needing to lock him out of the editing suite. In an early sequence in the documentary itself, Gortner can be seen giving camera directions and instructions on how to best film certain aspects of a revival meeting. As *Marjoe* editor Larry Silk explained in a short video posted by the Manhattan Edit Workshop on You Tube on December 31, 2015:

"He (Marjoe) was a very controlling personality. I was told to keep him out of the editing room, or else he would try and get in there to control what I was doing. He didn't trust anybody. For good reason, given his childhood. And he would be very seductive. When he did show up to look at the film, he came with a lawyer. He came in and looked at the film and he just loved it, he was just laughing, and his lawyer was laughing, too. They felt this ought to do the job and make him successful. And it won an Oscar."

Following its brief theatrical run, *Marjoe* sat mostly unseen while its star forged ahead with his career in film and television. After Donald Rurgoff, head of the Cinema 5 group which distributed the documentary, died in 1989, his catalogue of films was purchased by Columbia, who briefly issued *Marjoe* on VHS on their

RCA/Columbia Pictures Home Video label, though in a rather washed-out transfer that was taken not from the original negative but from an old distribution print. After RCA/Columbia dissolved in the early-nineties in the wake of a lawsuit filed against them by the NBC television network, Sarah Kernochan managed to buy back the rights to *Marjoe,* only to find herself stuck with the same deteriorating print which had been used on the VHS release. As good fortune would have it, when Kernochan was editing her Oscar-winning 2002 short documentary *Toth* in the same building where *Marjoe* had been processed almost thirty years earlier, she discovered the archives were still storing the original negative to the film, along with all the outtakes and original trailer, in perfect temperature-controlled conditions. Kernochan rescued her film in the nick of time, as the building were in the process of clearing out their archives and sending all of their old and unclaimed prints to the Library of Congress. *Marjoe* finally saw its DVD debut in the US on the Docurama label in January of 2006. Unfortunately, none of the original outtakes or any current input or update from Marjoe himself is included on the release, though it is still an enormous improvement on the old VHS and bootleg releases.

As an interesting aside, one of the cinematographers on *Marjoe*, Richard Pearce, whom Sarah Kernochan recalls as being particularly outspoken and critical of the way in which the documentary was casting a negative light on evangelists, would later go on to direct *Leap of Faith* (1992), a comedy starring Steve Martin as a phony faith healer stranded in a small town. It is a film which clearly owes a debt to *Marjoe* and indicates a distinct change in Pearce's attitude towards the subject.

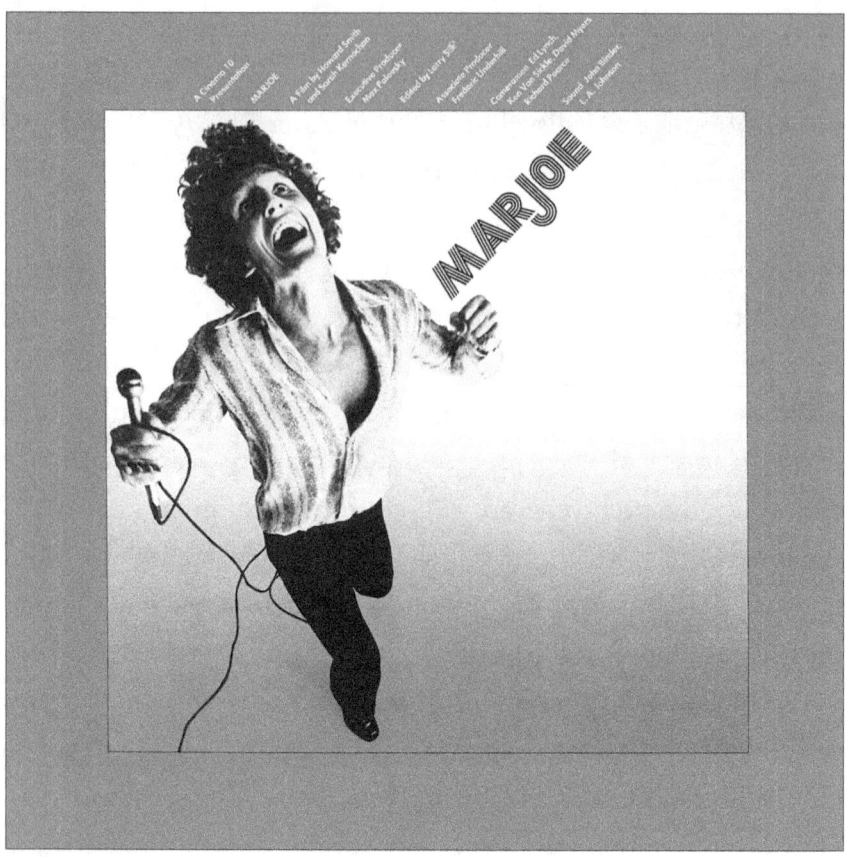

Original *Marjoe* soundtrack LP released on the Warner Brothers label in 1972.

SARAH KERNOCHAN ON MARJOE

New York born Sarah Kernochan is a filmmaker, screenwriter, musician and author. Apart from winning the Academy Award for Best Documentary Feature with her partner Howard Smith for *Marjoe*, she won a second Oscar in the Best Documentary Short Subject category for her 2002 film *Toth*, about the New York performance artist S. K. Thoth. Kernochan also wrote the screenplay for the controversial erotic drama *9½ Weeks* (1986), released two albums as a singer-songwriter for RCA Records in the 1970s (*House of Pain* and

Beat Around the Bush) and has authored the paranormal thriller *Jane Was Here* (2011, Grey Swan Press) and the erotic cult classic *Dry Hustle* (1976, Morrow), a fictionalized **exposé of the Times Square dance hall rackets.** *Dry Hustle* **was reprinted by** Professional Rabbit in 2010 as the sixth volume of their Erotic American Classics series.

How did the seed for the documentary first get planted? From what I understand Marjoe actually came to Howard Smith, your partner at the time, to pitch an article or documentary about himself?

He was not pitching a documentary at the point of our first meeting. Howard had a radio show on which he interviewed celebrities and various oddballs, and Marjoe presented himself as that kind of interesting oddball who thought it would be good to do a radio interview. He was seeking at that time to get some publicity. Marjoe knew very well that his backstory was fascinating to people and it was his kind of way to get people interested in him and he always carried around his album of all his newspaper clippings and photographs, especially to show to women that he wanted to seduce, because they would automatically be fascinated and feel sorry for him.

So he did the radio interview and Howard and I both being working colleagues and romantic partners had been long talking about doing a film together. I had just written my first screenplay and had gotten an agent, and when Howard brought home a photocopy of all of Marjoe's stuff I looked through it and said, "This is a documentary." So it was really our idea to do it that way, and Howard had connections to the one and only place that might have possibly had any interest in a documentary on that subject at the time, which was the only distributor who touched documentaries for theatrical distribution in those days. And as luck had it, they went for it so we didn't need to really shop the project around much, but Marjoe did accompany us to help sell it to the distributor's partners, who didn't know much about producing movies.

Anyway, we had dinner with this guy who was mega-rich and financing the film, and I pitched the story over our meal and then he turned to Marjoe and said "So, getting even with your parents, are you?"

So even at that early stage did you get the idea that Marjoe was looking upon the documentary as a way to cleanse his soul and get a lot of the lingering frustration from his childhood off his chest?
Well, that's what Marjoe says now, but at the time I think it was for the reason that he first came to Howard, because it was a way to get some attention for himself, and he wanted the attention so that he would not have to start anonymously in New York as an actor, which he found himself having to do when he first arrived. He wondered why he had to go to auditions and jump through all these hoops and find an agent. His thought was to get some publicity for himself based on his weird past, and then agents might be more willing to handle him or have an interest in him.

The other motive for Marjoe to do the documentary was not for any kind of revenge but to prevent himself from going back to preaching.

Kind of like insuring himself from ever being tempted by the preaching game again. No congregation would likely fall for his line after he put himself on film blowing the lid on the whole evangelism con game.
Well no one would have booked him, although he claimed—and I think accurately—that if he repented they would have loved to have taken him back because they love it when someone falls and then finds redemption.

There is a sequence you filmed for the documentary that was ultimately cut from the finished film, when a lady asks Marjoe at a party if he had ever stopped to consider that maybe he was genuinely gifted spiritually, and it seemed to take Marjoe aback somewhat and unsure of how to answer. Was that sequence cut at the request of Marjoe?

No, that was cut from the film purely because of running time constraints, although it was an interesting moment as it was one of the few times Marjoe was pushed about his duplicity, and he didn't take it very well. So even though it was cut for length, we also wondered what would be the point of showing Marjoe in a bad light, we thought the audience would do that instinctively so we wanted to make sure Marjoe was portrayed sympathetically to give it some balance.

Certainly the documentary, even though it fell into some distribution problems and wasn't seen for a number of years, did its bit in helping Marjoe establish a Hollywood career, as it wasn't long after Marjoe came out that he started appearing in films like Earthquake ***and in TV movies such as*** The Marcus–Nelson Murders ***and*** Pray for the Wildcats.

As soon as *Marjoe* came out in 1972 he was just the toast of the town in Hollywood, which was where he lived. He lived actually in the Venice area, I think, but he had basically been an L.A. guy for at least a decade prior. So he was on hand for all of the invitations he received to parties and premieres, it was a very popular movie and everyone wanted to meet him. And it was really one of the most heavily publicized movies of the year, which is kind of how we knew we were going to receive the Academy Award, because of everybody's interest in it, and the fact that someone came out and told the truth about the subject, and he had an extremely intriguing background. And people just really liked the film.

Marjoe says in the film that he would like to be either a rock star or an actor, and that helped him get a record deal right away. Though singing was not his forte, and that goes for in the film as well. But he was such a media star at that point that they thought they could establish him as a singer, and they gave him a really good producer as well. He had a lot of record industry push behind him with that album (*Bad But Not Evil*) but in the end he just didn't have the talent to make it work.

CHAPTER THREE

The Holy Hustler Hits Hollywood: The Marjoe Gortner Filmography

"I really wish I was getting it off as a rock star or an actor, which is something I have to get into."

— Marjoe Gortner (*Marjoe*)

BUILDING ON THE success and notoriety which the *Marjoe* documentary brought his way, Marjoe Gortner began to attract attention from Hollywood producers almost immediately. There can be little doubt that one of the primary reasons for film and television producers casting Marjoe in their projects was for exploitation of the name value which he had garnered through the documentary, particularly after its Oscar win. But it was certainly a two-way street, with Marjoe himself eager to establish a career as a performer, and a multi-faceted one at that. Less than two months after *Marjoe* premiered, in an interview with noted film critic Roger Ebert, he admitted he had been taking acting classes for over a year and had already turned down a couple of "weirdo" roles, an indication of how producers and casting agents were already visualizing potential onscreen characters for Gortner. While Marjoe's comment to Ebert seems to indicate an initial reluctance to accept any offers to portray disturbed or off–beat characters, his acting oeuvre would eventually encompass a large variety of roles which demonstrated strange and occasionally creepy behavior, not to mention reflective of his real–life past. It's possible that when the big studio offers and prominent leading men roles weren't forthcoming, Marjoe was forced to rethink his strategy and start trading in on his notoriety while he was still in the public eye.

While a lot of actors tend to focus on either film or television as their medium of choice (or circumstance), Marjoe's career continually traversed between the two, building an eclectic collection of work that attracted an audience to him from both mediums. The regular drive–in and grindhouse filmgoers no doubt became familiar with Marjoe's distinctive name and features while drinking, toking and making–out through such films as *Bobbie Joe and the Outlaw* (1976) and *Mausoleum* (1983), while TV viewers recognized him from a stream of guest appearances on episodic shows like *Police Story* (1973–1987) and *Fantasy Island* (1977–1984), usually playing a lowlife crim, drug addict or pimp, and soapie fans loved to despise him as the shyster fortune teller Vince Karlotti on *Falcon Crest* (1981–1990).

A Note about the filmography listings: Entries are listed chronologically according to date of release. Unless otherwise noted, all dates given refer to the original US theatrical release (or original US television air date, in relation to television movies).

THE MARCUS–NELSON MURDERS
USA/March 8, 1973/125 minutes
Director: Joseph Sargent
Writer: Abby Mann
Producers: Abby Mann & Matthew Rapf
Cast: Telly Savalas, Marjoe Gortner, José Ferrer, Ned Beatty, Lorraine Gary & Allen Garfield

The early–seventies was a fertile period for crime and police/detective shows on American television. Families of that generation spent many a night huddled around the box catching the latest episode of *Adam 12* (1968–1975), *Hawaii Five-O* (1968–1980), *The Rookies* (1972–1976), *The Streets of San Francisco* (1972–1977) and countless others. While later shows like *Starsky and Hutch* (1975–1979) helped shift the emphasis from drama to action, cop shows from earlier in the decade were much more character and story–based, with the cities they were set in often becoming an integral part of their appeal, and an essential character in the proceedings themselves.

Along with *Columbo* (1971–2003), one of the more unlikely detective show successes from this period was *Kojak*, which originally ran on the CBS network from 1973 to 1978 and starred Telly Savalas as the titular character, a tough and no–nonsense but understanding and compassionate New York City police lieutenant operating out of the 11th Precinct. Created by Abby Mann (who had won an Oscar with his screenplay for Stanley Kramer's classic 1961 war crimes drama *Judgement at Nuremberg*), Theo Kojak was first introduced to audiences in the TV pilot movie, *The Marcus–Nelson Murders*, which aired on CBS in their Thursday night slot on March 8, 1973, seven months before the series debuted in October. Mann also wrote the screenplay, and with a desire to explore racial prejudice and civil rights within the police force, gleaned a lot of his inspiration and reference points from Selwyn Raab's 1967 book *Justice in the Back Room*, which examined the case of George Whitmore, Jr., a young African American who in 1963 had been coerced by police into confessing to the murders of two young New York career women, a crime dubbed the Career Girl Murders and for which one Richard "Ricky" Robles would eventually be tried and convicted (Robles finally admitted to the crime in 1986). The character of Kojak himself was a composite of a number of authorities (and even a couple of journalists) who were involved in the Career Girls case. As played by Telly Savalas, with his shaved head (a rather bold fashion statement at the time), Greek heritage, Italian suits with flared shirt collars and fedora, Kojak made for an exotic television cop, but one that exuded a strong magnetism and sex appeal which clicked strongly with viewers. Savalas, already an established actor and star, became even more popular and iconic thanks to his role as Kojak, and even managed to launch something of a successful singing career on the back of it (his biggest hit coming with a spoken word cover of Bread's "If", which reached number one on the UK and Irish charts in March of 1975).

Told in an impressively gritty, docudrama style, *The Marcus–Nelson Murders* opens with a powerful point–of–view sequence depicting the rape and murder of two young New York women, Jo–Ann Marcus (Elizabeth Berger) and Kathy Nelson (Lora Kaye), by an unseen assailant. Six months later, in a more rundown area of Brooklyn, a black woman is raped and murdered while walking home at night, while another woman is attacked two weeks later but survives, pointing the finger at poor young black man Lewis Humes (Gene Woodbury), whom the arresting cops end up coercing a confession for the Marcus–Nelson murders out of. Lieutenant Kojak, the detective in charge of the Marcus–Nelson case, begins to doubt the validity of Humes' confession, uncovering a trail of police threats, beatings, denial of liberties and misconstruing of evidence to suit their own agenda.

With things not looking good for Humes, a break in the case comes when junkie Bobby Martin (Roger Robinson) is arrested for killing his dealer and immediately tries to cut a deal, telling the cops that he knows the truth behind the Marcus–Nelson murders. The real killer, Bobby claims, is his friend Teddy Hopper (Marjoe Gortner), a petty thief and junkie who lives in a small apartment with his older girlfriend Josie (Chita Rivera) and young son Joey. Though Kojak is aware of Teddy and his record, he clearly has something of a soft spot for him and doesn't peg him as a vicious killer. He also questions Bobbie's motives and willingness to give up his best friend at the drop of the hat, but the suspicions against Teddy grow when he takes an overdose of pills and has to be hospitalized on the same day that he was due to take a lie detector test over the killings. Bobby chillingly warns Kojak about Teddy: "Don't be taken in by that baby face and curly blonde hair. He iced 'em, he carved 'em up."

As the trial against Lewis Humes gets underway, Kojak's investigation into Teddy continues. His anger and distaste towards his fellow detectives and their willingness to send an innocent man to jail just to close a case also grows, especially since Humes is being tried for a case which he was initially in charge of. More determined than ever to uncover the truth behind the Marcus–Nelson murders, Kojak eventually backs Teddy into a corner and draws a confession out of him after planting some listening devices in Bobby's apartment and hearing Teddy talk about ways to beat a lie detector test. While Teddy's arrest sees Lewis Humes released and the murder charges against him dropped, his relief and freedom is short-lived, as he is quickly re-arrested and charged with one count of attempted rape, no doubt to be made an example out of for daring to speak out against the cops who forced the murder confession from him. Despite the lack of evidence, Humes is found guilty and sentenced to five years in prison, leaving Kojak disgusted and frustrated with his job and wanting to hand in his badge but driven on by his faith and belief in the basic ideal of the police force.

Troubled Teddy (Marjoe Gortner) gets the squeeze put on him by Lieutenant Theo Kojak (Telly Savalas).

Making his straight acting debut in the role of Teddy Hopper, Marjoe Gortner does not show up in *The Marcus–Nelson Murders* until well into the middle act. But when he does, he makes an immediate impression, and the introduction of his character certainly helps inject a bit more tension and drama into the final act, providing a nice balance with the courtroom scenes depicting the trial of Lewis Humes. Soft spoken with a boyish smile and a twinkle in his eyes, it's easy to see how Teddy's innocent features would help deflect suspicion away from him. There are some nice subtleties and nuances to Marjoe's performances, however. When Teddy is first brought into the police station for an interview and is met by Bobby telling him that he might as well come clean about the murders, he reacts with a bemused confusion, seemingly having no idea what Bobby is talking about. But there is one moment when Teddy's façade of innocence drops just for just a split-second, and his eyes shoot Bobby a look of pure hatred, like he cannot believe that his supposed friend has dared to turn on him. It's a great moment from Marjoe, one that you have to be quick to spot, but it hints beautifully at Teddy's hidden psychotic undertow. As the pressure from the cops mounts, Teddy's demeanor starts to change, his early calm manner giving way to a more nervous and jittery body language, sweaty complexion and a sharp increase in his heroin habit. Once again, Marjoe handles the transition of his character with some nice subtle touches, slowly building Teddy up until he has you on edge with anticipation, bracing for the eruption of his anger which you feel could come at any moment (which makes his eventual low-key, matter-of-fact confession to Kojak all the more surprising and effective).

With his role being more of a strong supporting player than a lead, *The Marcus-Nelson Murders* provided Marjoe with the perfect entry point for his acting career, without the pressure of having to carry a whole movie on his shoulders. It proved very successful for him, as *The Marcus-Nelson Murders* was, and indeed remains, a highly-regarded television movie from that period, with Marjoe's performance frequently noted amongst its highlights. Of course, he was in strong company with Telly Savalas in the lead, giving us a much tougher and grounded Theo Kojak than what we would see in the subsequent television series (where the character would develop his famous penchant for lollipops and the phrase "Who loves ya, baby?"). Also delivering nice performances in *The Marcus–Nelson Murders* are Ned Beatty and William C. Watson as racist, amoral detectives, José Ferrer as the attorney who represents Lewis Hume in court, and a particularly appealing supporting role from Lorraine Gary as a troubled former flame of Kojak's who briefly comes back into his life after a chance meeting in a supermarket (a very endearing and nicely written and performed scene). Gary of course would soon become famous for her role in Steven Spielberg's *Jaws* (1975) and two of its three sequels, and would also appear in Marjoe's next TV movie, *Pray for the Wildcats* (1974).

The Marcus–Nelson Murders was directed by Joseph Sargent, who received a Directors Guild of America award for his work here, as well as an Emmy. They are awards well deserved, as he delivered a film that is not only rich in drama and character but, thanks to help from cinematographer Mario Tosi, captures a visually arresting and baroque vision of a grotty and depressing New York City, particularly the crumbling, abandoned tenement buildings of Brownsville, Brooklyn. Sargent was a prolific director of TV movies, with one of his more notorious efforts being *The Night that Panicked America* (1975), which dramatized Orson Welles' infamous 1938 radio adaptation of H. G. Wells' *War of the Worlds*, a radio broadcast which sent some parts of America into a panicked frenzy when they believed the show—presented in an on-the-spot, newsflash style approach—was covering a genuine invasion of the Earth by Martians. Sargent also directed a number of interesting theatrical features throughout his career, including the science-fiction thriller *Colossus: The Forbin Project* (1970), the exciting Southern moonshine action flick *White Lightning* (1973) with Burt Reynolds, and the incredibly tense and well-constructed crime thriller *The Taking of Pelham One Two Three* (1974). Trash film fans also know him for the sequel *Jaws: The Revenge* (1987), widely considered the worst of the *Jaws* films but an enjoyably ludicrous movie in its own right (and a film which re-united Sargent with one of the stars from *The Marcus-Nelson Murders*, Lorraine Gary).

PRAY FOR THE WILDCATS
USA/January 23, 1974/100 minutes
Director: Robert Michael Lewis
Writer: Jack Turley
Producer: Anthony Wilson
Cast: **Andy Griffith, William Shatner, Robert Reed, Marjoe Gortner, Angie Dickinson, Janet Margolin & Lorraine Gary**

Though they first started appearing with increasing regularity by the mid-1960s, it wasn't until early in the following decade that the American made for television movie really came of age. Not only was Steven Spielberg making his name on the small screen at this point in time, with the excellent 73-minute *Columbo* episode "Murder by the Book" from 1971, as well as helming his breakthrough TV movie hit *Duel* in the same year, but producers and studios were really starting to realize the potential, both financially and creative, of the format. The first half of the seventies saw an amazing stream of memorable TV movies emerge from not only the big networks, who would produce the movies in-house, but also from independent filmmakers, who would finance the productions themselves before selling them to the networks, both national and regional.

Directed by Robert Michael Lewis, who cut his filmmaking teeth on many episodes of *The Mod Squad* (1968–1973) and *McMillan & Wife* (1971–1977), as well as the excellent TV movie *The Astronaut* (1972), *Pray for the Wildcats* starts out as a male bonding session before leading its characters into a fight for both emotional and physical survival. Sam Farragut (Andy Griffith) is a successful but controlling Californian business executive who refuses to sign a big contract with an advertising agency unless the three men involved in the campaign agree to join him on a motorbike trip to the Baja desert, to prove their mental and physical toughness and worthiness for his business, as well as to scout out the location for a potential commercial. While art designer Terry Maxon (Marjoe Gortner) and company man Paul McIlvain (Robert Reed) are receptive to the adventure, Warren Summerfield (William Shatner) is less enthusiastic. Claiming to be too busy to take off on an impromptu road trip, the real reason for Summerfield's reluctance to join the others is his recent firing from his agency (which his co-workers do not yet know about), which has sent him into a suicidal depression. Summerfield finally relents, but only after taking out a large life insurance policy on himself, after which he plans to commit suicide while on the trip and make it look like a road accident in order for his wife (Lorraine Gary) to collect the money to ensure a comfortable future for herself.

The Wildcats (Left to Right: Marjoe Gortner, Robert Reed, Andy Griffith and William Shatner) suit-up for the adventure of a middle-aged lifetime in *Pray for the Wildcats*.

Decked out in customized, matching black leather jackets with "Baja Wildcats" stamped on them in white lettering, it isn't long before Maxon, McIlvain and Summerfield begin to realize that Farragut is a ruthless and rather unbalanced individual whose dangerous behavior could lead to serious consequences for both himself and them. The first major sign of trouble comes when the foursome stop to wet their whistles in a grimy little dive bar out in the middle of the desert, where the drunken Farragut leers and applauds wildly as a young blonde hippy girl with bell–bottom jeans and crop–top dances by herself to the music playing. Not content with merely watching, Farragut decides to get up and dance closely with the girl, something which her boyfriend Michael (Robert 'Skip' Burton) clearly doesn't appreciate. A brief fight breaks out between the two, which Farragut seems to be winning before the scuffle is broken up. The four men jump back on their bikes and continue on the journey deeper into Baja, with Summerfield at one point contemplating riding his bike over a high cliff top, while Farragut continues to stew over the incident back at the bar. When he and Maxon come across the same young couple on the beach, Farragut decides to humiliate Michael by offering him $100 to sleep with his girlfriend. "I'm a hippy with money", Farragut tells the disgusted Michael, before another fight breaks out between the pair. As Maxon looks on helplessly, Farragut picks up an axe that Michael had been chopping firewood with and chases the boy off down the beach, before returning and swinging the axe into the radiator on the couple's camper van.

When the Wildcats ride into a small town the following day, they are met by a sheriff who tells them that Michael has been found dead in the desert, while his girlfriend is in hospital clinging to life. The couple had been found some miles away from their camper van, which was unable to be started due to the broken radiator. Motorbike tracks found around the vehicle make the sheriff suspicious of the four visitors, but Farragut proclaims his innocence, claiming that he had not been in contact with the couple since the incident in the bar. Maxon, worried about losing the potential contract with Farragut if he speaks up, remains silent, though Summerfield and McIlvain suspect he knows more than he is saying. When news breaks that Michael's girlfriend has died without regaining consciousness and identifying Michael's attacker, Farragut and Maxon decide to hightail it back home before any new evidence comes to light. Summerfield, using his anger to shake off his depression, is determined to make Farragut face the consequences of his actions, and he takes off in pursuit. As Farragut and Summerfield face off with a chase along the ridge of a cliff, Farragut loses control and sends himself and his bike flying over the edge to his fiery death below.

Returning to the U.S. with Farragut's body, the three men are greeted by their respective partners – while Summerfield and his wife seem to have garnered a new lease of life and renewed optimism for the future from the ordeal, McIlvain's wife informs her shocked husband that she is leaving him, and Maxon's girlfriend Krissie (Janet Margolin), who had informed her partner before he left that she was expecting with his child, tells Maxon that she is no longer pregnant, suggesting that she has had an abortion while he was away.

At 100 minutes, *Pray for the Wildcats* runs somewhat longer than the typical TV movie of its time (which usually clocked in at around the 80–minute mark). Much of the extended runtime can be explained by the lengthy sequences of motorbikes kicking up sand as they race across the Baja desert, which do provide a nice view of the scenic locations and motorbike lovers will enjoy watching the Kawasaki and Triumph machines in action, but the film's pace could have definitely been improved by trimming some of these scenes (though these motorbike sequences do give composer Fred Myrow the chance to inject the soundtrack with some cool acid/fuzz guitar, a familiar sound in classic biker films).

While all four male leads put in good performances, it is William Shatner and Andy Griffith who steal the show here. Shatner is in fine form as the suicidal advertising executive, now out of a job and facing a future without income and a mounting string of debts, while Griffith, who was 48 at the time, plays well against type as the leering, hedonistic sociopath who needs to control all those around him, and lets nothing get in the way of what he wants. Griffith really does give a creepy, menacing performance, and seems especially effective when compared to the role he was at that point best known for, Sheriff Andy Taylor in the long–running television series *The Andy Griffith Show* (1960–1968). The female performers in *Pray for the Wildcats* are unfortunately not given a whole lot to do, though Angie Dickinson and Lorraine Gary share a nice scene together, when Dickinson's Nancy confesses to Gary's Lila about the affair she is having with her husband (a revelation that comes as little surprise to her), and also tries to raise concerns about her fears that Warren is planning to kill himself (a fear that the in–denial Lila brushes aside).

Though it is not very developed or complex, the character of Maxon does give Marjoe a couple of chances to flex his acting muscles in this early role. At least a decade younger than the other three men, Maxon is clearly the up–and–coming hotshot of the advertising team, with high career ambitions which makes him the one to be most easily manipulated by Farragut (who brands Maxon a "maverick"). One of Marjoe's key moments in the film takes place when we see him in his home studio, as he proudly shows his girlfriend Krissie a very colorful, Peter Max inspired painting that he hopes Farragut will use for his campaign. His excitement is tempered somewhat when Krissie announces that she is pregnant with his child, a piece of news that Maxon is unsure of which way to take. While Maxon seems happy in his relationship with Krissie, he clearly feels a little trapped by the thought of becoming a father, and no doubt thinks the responsibilities involved in having a child might slow down his career development. Maxon is hungry for success and the presumed happiness, wealth and status which he feels it will bring him. "I'm gonna get me a piece of the American Dream!", Maxon exalts to his companions in the bar, with a wild–eyed fervor that instantly recalls Marjoe's evangelical sermons. The experience of the Baja road trip obviously effects Maxon deeply and helps him to mature emotionally, as we find out when he is reunited with Krissie and he informs her that he is looking forward to becoming a father to her child. Unfortunately, his awakening has come a bit too late, as Krissie has already acted upon Maxon's initial reluctance to embrace fatherhood and has terminated her pregnancy. While there is no indication that their relationship is about to end, it is clear that the dynamic of it has been changed, not just because of the abortion but because of the awakening which Maxon has experienced due to his primal adventure in the desert.

With a screenplay by prolific television writer Jack Turley (*The Fugitive, Lost in Space, The Mod Squad, Hawaii Five-O* and many more), *Pray for the Wildcats* does an admirable job of balancing action and drama with character, and examining the psyche of the 1970s American male coming to grips with the fact that they are not as young as they used to be, and feeling increasingly irrelevant in a youth–obsessed world ("Where do good–looking aging boys go?", McIlvain asks of Summerfield at one point).

THE GUN AND THE PULPIT
USA/April 3, 1974/74 minutes
Director: Daniel Petrie
Writer: William Bowers
Producers: Paul Junger Witt, Paul Maslansky & Tony Thomas
Cast: Marjoe Gortner, Slim Pickens, David Huddleston, Geoffrey Lewis, Estelle Parsons, Pamela Sue Martin & Jeff Corey

After impressive supporting performances in two television movies, Marjoe was given the chance to prove himself as a lead actor in yet another made–for–TV production, this time in a role that was much more reflective of his real life past. Based on the 1972 novel *The Fastest Gun in the Pulpit* by Jack Ehrlich, *The Gun and the Pulpit* was originally intended as a pilot movie for a proposed television series which unfortunately failed to materialize.

The Gun and the Pulpit begins with gunfighter Ernie Parsons (Marjoe Gortner) hanging from a tree and about to be lynched for the supposed killing of another criminal. When the head of the posse who have caught him (played by Jeff Corey) asks Ernie if he would like to be read a passage from the Bible before he swings, he responds with disgust: "No thanks. I don't want anyone praying over me. I don't believe in that stuff." Fortunately for the condemned man, he is saved at the last moment by the lies of a pretty young blonde woman who is smitten with him. Though saved from the noose, Ernie is ordered to leave town without delay ("We don't want no fast guns in this town").

As Ernie takes off on horseback across the desert, he fortuitously stumbles across the body of a preacher who has been shot in the back. Searching the dead man's clothes, he discovers not only a bag of gold coins but a letter from a resident of Castle Walk, a small town in Arizona, begging the preacher to come and instill some faith and guidance into the citizens, despite the fact that no one in town has ever met the preacher before. This triggers an idea in Ernie's head, and he quickly changes into the dead preacher's clothing, hops upon his horse and heads straight for Castle Walk, arriving in town just in time to clumsily preside over a funeral for a man who has been murdered on the orders from Mr. Ross (David Huddleston), a ruthless businessman who runs the town with a tight grip and has all of its citizens—men, women and children alike—quaking in fear at the mere mention of his name.

Now posing as Reverend Frank Fleming (the name of the dead preacher), Ernie is one person who is not afraid of Mr. Ross and his goons, and he promises to free the residents of Castle Walk from his reign of terror, taking a particular interest in Sally Underwood (Pamela Sue Martin), the pretty young daughter of the man who has just been buried. "We're all sinners, or about to be", Ernie tells his new flock, before his first Sunday sermon ends up in a gunfight, with Ernie shooting dead one of Mr. Ross' henchmen, who has been sent into the church to intimidate him, a ploy which clearly backfires. Though the residents of Castle Walk find the methods of their new preacher to be unconventional to say the least, they are willing to put their faith and trust in him, although the elderly Billy One–Eye (Slim Pickens) soon cottons on to his real identity, but is willing to keep the secret to himself since Ernie's presence in town has clearly been a positive thing.

Mr. Ross, however, is not happy with having the new gun–to–tin' preacher snubbing his nose at his authority and instilling defiance into the townsfolk, and with his own henchmen unable to do the job, he calls in hired gunman Jason McCoy (Geoffrey Lewis) to take care of the problem. Unfortunately, their showdown in the center of town ends in a stalemate when both men draw and completely miss their targets! McCoy takes this as a sign from above and quickly decides to skip town, once again leaving Mr. Ross to deal with the problem on his own. When Ernie is lassoed by Mr. Ross' men and left for dead after being dragged by horse through the desert, his body bouncing off rocks and cacti, Sally discovers him unconscious and nurses Ernie back to health, agreeing to go along with his plan to pretend he has been killed in the assault. Presumed dead by the townsfolk, Ernie sneaks out each night under the cloak of darkness to torment Mr. Ross and his men, tearing down the sign above the entrance to his ranch and throwing dynamite onto his property, before resurrecting himself for a big Sunday service, during which Mr. Ross appears and offers a truce.

With the town now seemingly at peace, Ernie and Sally prepare to marry, but just as the ceremony gets underway they get word that Mr. Ross has gone back on his word and double-crossed them, and is planning to ambush the wedding. Ernie urges the frightened townsfolk to finally stand up for themselves and fight, and the streets of Castle Walk are soon alive with gunfire, with Ernie emerging victorious after shooting Mr. Ross dead in a boarding house room and urging his henchmen to give up their futile fight. Though now free to marry Sally, Ernie is convinced by Billy One-Eye that it would be a sham marriage and unfair to Sally if she didn't know the real truth about him and his past. Ernie reluctantly agrees and, without saying a word to Sally, rides out of town and into the desert, where he comes across another preacher who is himself heading into Castle Walk to investigate all the chaos that has been going down. Though the preacher is onto Ernie's ruse, he tells the gunslinger that perhaps he has found the work he was destined to do with his life. Uncertain, Ernie hands over the bag of gold coins that he had stolen from the preacher's body, requesting it be passed onto Sally, before riding off into the horizon and adventures unknown.

The Gun and the Pulpit was written by William Bowers (a noted writer of westerns) and directed by Daniel Petrie, a triple primetime Emmy winner whose feature film career included the racial drama *A Raison in the Sun* (1961) with Sidney Poitier, the lycanthrope TV movie *Moon of the Wolf* (1972), the sci–fi adventure *The Neptune Factor* (1973) and the gritty urban crime drama *Fort Apache, the Bronx* (1980) starring Paul Newman.

Though it bears all the hallmarks of a low–budget television production (it was produced by actor Danny Thomas' production company), *The Gun and the Pulpit* is overall a fairly entertaining though completely harmless and thoroughly predictable western melodrama. It's easy to see why it wasn't picked–up as a regular series—westerns were not the most *en vogue* genre on television at the time—even though you could see the potential in the further adventures of Ernie Parsons/Reverend Frank Fleming. And it's Marjoe Gortner's performance that provides the film with its most valuable asset. Cocky and confident without being annoyingly arrogant, Marjoe really creates a likeable character whose genuine willingness to help the people of Castle Walk makes you overlook and forgive the sins of his past and the charade he is carrying out. Of course, you definitely get the sense that one of the main reasons he is sticking around is to act on his lusty ambitions towards young Sally, but he keeps his libido pretty much PG–rated and never comes across as threatening or a sleaze, more a horny but harmless conman who spontaneously takes on Mr. Ross and his men as much for his own amusement as he does out of any sense of moral righteousness.

Supporting Marjoe are a number of actors who all turn in likeable performances. Pamela Sue Martin had already made something of a name for herself as both a model and one of the stars of *The Poseidon Adventure* (1972), and she brings a nice mixture of innocence and sexual curiosity to her role as Sally. Martin would later go on to establish herself as something of a teen idol thanks to her television role as teen detective Nancy Drew in *The Hardy Boys/Nancy Drew Mysteries* (1977–1978), before ditching her wholesome image with a photospread in *Playboy* (July 1978) and a recurring role on the popular nighttime soap *Dynasty* (1981–1984), where she played Fallon Carrington Colby.

There's also Geoffrey Lewis, who counted his actor/singer daughter Juliette amongst his ten children and who regularly worked for Clint Eastwood during the 1970s. As gunslinger Jason McCoy, Lewis' role in *The Gun and the Pulpit* is brief but memorable, thanks to the actor's unique, hardened face and New Jersey drawl. Slim Pickens is always fun to watch, even if he is playing the type of western character he could play in his sleep, and Jeff Corey was an interesting character actor who became a well-respected acting teacher after he became blacklisted by Hollywood in the 1950s during the anti-Communist scare. Acting roles started being offered to him again in the mid-sixties, and he would go on to play roles in such noted films as *Seconds* (1966), *In Cold Blood* (1967), *The Boston Strangler* (1968), *True Grit* (1968), and *Butch Cassidy and the Sundance Kid* (1968).

While *The Gun and the Pulpit* may not have led to the hoped-for series, it showed that while his skills as an actor were still developing, Marjoe definitely had the screen presence and natural charisma to handle a lead role, though in his next film he would take a back seat to a number of big Hollywood stars in a movie that promised to make the cinemas themselves rumble and shake, and would ultimately prove to be the biggest commercial hit of his on-screen career.

EARTHQUAKE
USA/November 15, 1974/121 minutes
Director: Mark Robson
Writers: George Fox & Mario Puzo
Producer: Mark Robson
Cast: **Charlton Heston, Ava Gardner, George Kennedy, Lorne Greene, Geneviève Bujold, Richard Roundtree, Marjoe Gortner, Barry Sullivan & Victoria Principal**

Whether man-made or an act of nature, disaster—or the ominous threat of it—has always been a popular and dramatic situation to depict on film. The bigger the looming cataclysm, the more exciting the drama. In much the same way as we stay glued to the news channel whenever some big terrorist attack, earthquake or tsunami hits a part of the world, we become intrigued by the humanity of the event, grateful it is not happening to us, yet putting ourselves in the same situation, wondering how we would react in the face of such mad panic and blind terror.

Disasters of both fact and fiction hit our movie screens countless times prior to the 1970s, whether it was a giant rogue star slamming into Earth as in George Pal's classic *When Worlds Collide* (1951), a passenger plane soaring through the skies without a pilot in *Zero Hour!* (1957), or the depiction of the mighty Titanic sinking to the bottom of the icy Atlantic on its maiden voyage in *A Night to Remember* (1958). However, if we were to narrow down the disaster film to a period when it was at its most popular and genre-defining, it would clearly have to be the 1970s. Indeed, the decade kicked-off with the biggest disaster imaginable, as the Earth was burned to a cinder at the cataclysmic finale of *Beneath the Planet of the Apes* (1970). But the birth of the modern disaster film is widely—and rightly—regarded to be George Seaton's *Airport* (1970). Released in March of 1970, *Airport* was based on the novel of the same name by British/Canadian writer Arthur Hailey, which was first published in 1968 by Doubleday. The mass-market paperback printing of *Airport* in 1969 would, appropriately enough, become a familiar sight on airport newsstands around the globe, as the novel became a best-seller, and seemed perfectly suited to reading while waiting in the departure lounge or on long cross-country or international flights. By 1977, according to Alice Hackett's *Eighty Years of Bestsellers* published that year, over five million copies of *Airport* had been sold in paperback to that point. Published at a time when air travel was still considered to be rather exciting and somewhat exotic (as captured in Susan Raye's 1971 pop hit *L.A. International Airport*), *Airport*'s combining of multiple soap-opera storylines, with some traditional thriller elements, and the dramatic setting, made it a natural for the big screen treatment. Universal Pictures soon snapped up the rights, hiring writer/director Seaton to turn Hailey's book into a filmable screenplay and cramming it with a roll call of stars that included Burt Lancaster, Dean Martin, George Kennedy, Van Heflin, Jean Seberg, Jacqueline Bisset, Helen Hayes and more. It set a casting template for the disaster movies to follow—topline it with a couple of big names who are still near the peak of their star power, then fill the supporting cast with a group of former stars for the nostalgia crowd and a few young up and comers to appeal to the all-important youth audience.

Considering how progressively outrageous its subsequent sequels and the disaster genre on the whole would become, the plot of *Airport* is really quite low-key, with the drama and romance pushed well to the fore, while the tension was provided by events both on the ground (with a Boeing 707 snow-bogged during a blizzard on the runway of Chicago's Lincoln International Airport) and in the air (with a depressed, out-of-work demolitions expert threatening to blow-up a 707 in flight). The majority of the film's 137 running time was taken up with the personal lives, scandals and woes of the main cabin and cockpit crew, airport staff and passengers, including imminent marriage breakdowns, randy married pilots getting their chief stewardess pregnant, and a little old lady who is an habitual stowaway.

Despite its leisurely pace and soap opera plot, *Airport* proved to be a huge hit with audiences, taking in over $100 million at the American box-office, a very impressive figure at the time. Though Lancaster dismissed the film as *"The biggest piece of junk ever made"* (in *The Montreal Gazette,* March 8, 1971), it was nominated for ten Academy Awards, including Best Picture, Best Writing (Adapted Screenplay), Best Cinematography and Best Original Score. It eventually ended up winning only one (Helen Hayes for Best Supporting Actress), but it proved that the big-scale disaster movie could bring both financial success and prestige to a studio. It was then that Irwin Allen would enter the picture and soon make the disaster genre his own, becoming so synonymous with it that he would forever be known as "The Master of Disaster."

Allen, of course, was already an established and well-known figure to fantasy film fans, as director of the dinosaur adventure *The Lost World* (1960), but mostly as the creator and producer for a quartet of classic science-fiction and fantasy television shows of the 1960s: *Voyage to the Bottom of the Sea* (1964–1968), *Lost in Space* (1965–1968), *The Time Tunnel* (1966–1967) and *Land of the Giants* (1968–1970). His knowledge and first-hand experience working with miniatures and other special effects on those shows would have no doubt given him confidence when he turned his attention to putting *The Poseidon Adventure* (1972) onto the big screen for 20th Century Fox.

Based on a pulpy 1969 adventure novel by Paul Gallico, *The Poseidon Adventure* was a much more-fast-paced and rousing disaster movie than *Airport*. Directed by respected Englishman Ronald Neame, the plot of *The Poseidon Adventure* is centered around the titular aged luxury liner, SS Poseidon, on her final journey from New York to Athens and the scrapyard. As the Poseidon's final haul of passengers celebrate New Year's Eve, an enormous wave, triggered by an underwater earthquake, overturns the ocean liner, leaving a small band of survivors trapped inside below the waterline. Led by Frank Scott, a radical young Reverend played by Gene Hackman, the group attempt to make their way up through the bottom of the Poseidon, in the chance that a part of the hull will still be above the surface, and a rescue team would be awaiting them. Among those joining him on his treacherous adventure are Ernest Borgnine and Stella Stevens (as a gruff ex-cop and his one-time hooker wife), Roddy McDowall (as a dining room attendant), Shelly Winters and Jack Albertson (as a retired couple heading to Israel to meet their small grandson for the first time), Pamela Sue Martin (as a teenager stuck with her bratty, know-it-all younger brother) and Carol Lynley as the Poseidon's young lounge singer.

Partly filmed aboard the RMS Queen Mary (whose encounter with a near-100-foot rogue wave in December of 1942 provided the initial inspiration for Gallico's novel), *The Poseidon Adventure* had a near-perfect balance of exaggerated melodrama and exciting peril, punctuated by still-impressive stunts and set-pieces, and featuring enjoyable performances from most of the cast (particularly Hackman, Borgnine, Stevens and Winters). Launched with an aggressive marketing campaign, the film became an enormous box-office hit when it was released in December of 1972, helped along by the theme song *The Morning After*, which in the movie was sung by Renne Armand (providing a vocal double for Carol Lynley), but became a chart success when recorded by Maureen McGovern and released as a single in 1973.

Building on the success of *The Poseidon Adventure*, the disaster film would hit its peak in 1974, with the release of three big studio pictures: *Earthquake, The Towering Inferno and Airport 1975* (which, despite its title, was released in October of 1974). Depicting the lead-up to a massive quake which causes catastrophic damage to the majority of Los Angeles, as well as the struggle for survival in the face of its aftermath, *Earthquake* had perhaps the most unbelievable lead casting of all the big 70s disaster movies, with Lorne Greene cast as Ava Gardner's father, despite the fact that Greene was only seven years older than Gardner. Gardner, playing the jealous and bitter wife of former football star Charlton Heston, puts in a hysterical and overly dramatic performance, running to daddy and faking overdoses in order to get attention and her way, but the rest of *Earthquake*'s cast is equally quirky and fun. There's Richard Roundtree as a struggling Evel Knievel wannabe in tight black leathers with bright orange lightning bolts (he looks like a blaxploitation riff on the classic Spider-Man villain, Electro). Other faces appearing in *Earthquake* include George Kennedy, Barry Sullivan, Geneviève Bujold, Victoria Principal and Walter Matthau in a cameo as a barfly (credited as Walter Matuschanskayasky).

And then of course we have Marjoe Gortner. In his first theatrical feature film (aside from the *Marjoe* documentary), Gortner plays the rather androgynously-named Jody Joad, a manager at a neighborhood grocery store who is also a member of the National Guard. When we first meet Jody at his store, he seems friendly and eager to please, if a little manic in his demeanor. When pretty young customer Rosa Amici (future *Dallas* star Victoria Principal, wearing a black afro wig) realizes she does not have enough money to cover her groceries, Jody graciously allows her to pay the balance next time she is in (try finding a grocery store that will allow you to do that these days!). Moments later, his angrier side emerges when he tries to get grizzled patrol cop Lou Slade (George Kennedy) to break–up a group of Hari Krishna *"freaks"* who are congregating and chanting outside of his store. *"You got something against religion?"*, he asks Jody in a moment which seems to deliberately play on Gortner's real–life past. Jody races home after word comes across the radio that the National Guard is being called up to help deal with the expected panic that is likely to ensue once the predicted "big one" hits the area (amusingly, he strips off his apron and immediately vacates the check–out register upon hearing the call–up notice, leaving his customers confused and stranded).

Returning to his tiny boarding house room in what looks like a rundown part of town, Jody finds himself being accosted and followed up the apartment stairs by three neighbors, who make fun of him for having photos of male bodybuilders taped to his walls. The ridicule of Jody continues when he emerges dressed in his National Guard uniform with a bad wig sitting on his head in order to cover his long curly locks and look more suitably military. Jody ignores the taunts but gets even with his tormentors when he reappears much later in the movie, machine–gunning them down in the streets after he catches them looting jewelry stores in the wake of the devastating quake. His National Guard unit also comes across Rosa while she is trying to empty the cash register in an abandoned store, and after taking personal responsibility for her, Jody lures her into a ruined building and puts the hard word on the terrified young lady, one moment lavishing her with the stolen jewelry confiscated from his executed neighbors, the next minute condemning her for wearing a tight–fitting t-shirt (*"Only a whore would wear something like that!"*). Clearly a psychotic whose impulses and pent–up anger and frustrations have been unleashed by the freedom he feels the National Guard uniform grants him, Jody is eventually taken care of by cop Slade, who comes to the aid of Rosa after having a tense encounter with Jody in the street. Killed by a bullet to the head which hits with such force it knocks his wig clean off, our last image of Jody is of him lying on his back, his lifeless eyes open and staring off into the dark void of death. It's a fate that would await several of Marjoe's on–screen characters again in the years ahead.

Co–written by *Godfather* (1972) scribe Mario Puzo and helmed by Mark Robson, director of the highly entertaining war adventure *Von Ryan's Express* (1965) and the soap opera showbiz drama *Valley of the Dolls* (1967), the special effects in *Earthquake* range from very impressive to laughably ludicrous. Animated drops of blood flying at the camera (during the scene when a packed elevator crashes to the ground) and an obvious lens distortion trick to depict city buildings swaying in the quake would have seemed ineffective even at the time, but on the other hand, there is some terrific miniature and model work on display, particularly in the destruction of the Mulholland Dam and the subsequent flooding which ensues (it is far more convincing than a similar scene in Richard Donner's later *Superman: The Movie* from 1978).

The Holy Hustler Hits Hollywood

The disturbed Jody (a be–wigged Marjoe Gortner) forces himself upon poor Rosa (Victoria Principal) in *Earthquake*.

"ATTENTION! This motion picture will be shown in the startling new multi–dimension of Sensurround. Please be aware that you will feel as well as see and hear realistic effects such as might be experienced in an actual earthquake. The management assumes no responsibility for the physical or emotional reactions of the individual viewer."—Theater Notice for Earthquake.

The biggest special effects in *Earthquake*, however, was not visual but aural. To enhance the experience for the audience, Universal Studios and loudspeaker manufacturer Cerwin–Vega combined to create Sensurround, a new sound system featuring a low frequency noise generator that added simulated rumble and vibrations to the movie, effectively rattling the audience in their seats during the earthquake sequences. Costing $2,000 to install in each cinema that wanted to use the process, Sensurround was certainly effective as a cinematic gimmick (in the vein of 3D in the 1950s) and an enormous benefit to the marketing campaign for *Earthquake*, yet the process failed to really take–off, and was used by Universal in only three other films: *Midway* (1976), *Rollercoaster* (1977) and the pilot episode of *Battlestar Galactica* (1978), which was released theatrically in many countries (including Australia, where I saw it in Sensurround on its first run, the only film I've been lucky to experience in that process).

When *Earthquake* was sold to television in 1976, Universal brought in editor Gene Palmer to shoot around twenty minutes of new footage in order to flesh the film out so it could be screened in two ninety–minute instalments over subsequent evenings, debuting on NBC on Sunday, September 26 and Monday, September 27. Shooting additional scenes for the television broadcasts of feature films became something of a trend in the 1970s, with Universal also adding new footage to several of their other titles from this period, including *Two–Minute Warning* (1976) and *Airport '79: The Concord* (1979). For the *Earthquake* reshoots, Marjoe Gortner was brought back to the studio to film some new sequences that further emphasized Jody's obsession with Victoria Principal's Rosa character. The new footage shows Jody following Rosa home after their meeting at the grocery store. As Rosa takes a shower and changes into a pink bathrobe, Jody can be seen at one of the windows, peeping in on the young woman as she changes and does her make-up, a big leering grin on his face (it's quite laughable how clear and blatant Jody's presence is at the window). Jody then knocks on her door and tells Rosa that the National Guard has called him up and he just wanted to make sure she was alright, and despite the fact that he admits to following her home to find out where she lives, Rosa not only invites the creepy grocery clerk inside but even asks him out to a movie (which Jody stupidly declines)! Another new shot added shows Jody walking home after his meeting with Rosa and stopping to admire a burning building and remarking how beautiful it looks to those standing by, just in case viewers needed any more hints about what a psycho he is.

Victoria Principal and Marjoe Gortner share a lighter moment between takes on the set of *Earthquake*.

While many extended TV cuts of films simply edited in footage that was originally filmed during the movie's production but left on the cutting room floor before release, it's clear from Marjoe's look (and Victoria Principal's altered afro wig) that these new scenes were filmed at a later date (apparently, the film's original director Mark Robson refused to come in to shoot the new footage). For the movie's initial television broadcast, audiences in New York and Los Angeles were able to tune into an FM radio station to hear the Sensurround audio (this was long before home theatre surround sound was a thing). The audio gimmick no doubt helped the broadcast become a huge success, with *TV Guide* reporting that the first installment garnered a staggering 41 share of television audiences.

BOBBIE JO AND THE OUTLAW
USA/March 26, 1976/89 minutes
Director: Mark L. Lester
Writer: Vernon Zimmerman
Producers: Steve Broidy, Mark L. Lester & Merrie Lynn Ross (as Lynn Ross)
Cast: Marjoe Gortner, Lynda Carter, Jesse Vint, Merrie Lynn Ross, Belinda Balaski & Gerrit Graham

With the release of *Bobbie Jo and the Outlaw*, Marjoe really started to find his niche as a leading man in low–to–medium–budget exploitation and grindhouse films, a career path he would pretty much follow for the next ten years, alternating his appearances in genre cinema with continuing guest spots on episodic television programs that helped keep his name and face in a more mainstream public eye than the audience that watched his movies from behind a windscreen at the local drive-in.

Originally conceived by director Mark L. Lester as an old–fashioned western to be titled *Desperado* (inspired by Lester hearing the classic Eagles song on the car radio one day), *Bobbie Jo and the Outlaw* eventually developed into a more modern updating of the Bonnie and Clyde mythos, with elements of the Southern 'good ole boy' action genre that was popular with drive-in audiences of the day (epitomized by films like Jack Sargent's *White Lightning* [1973] starring Burt Reynolds), as well as retaining some of the western flavor as initially envisioned by Lester.

Lyle Wheeler (Marjoe Gortner) teaches Bobbie Jo Baker (Lynda Carter) how to shoot a pistol on this American lobby card for *Bobbie Jo and the Outlaw.*

Bobbie Jo Baker (Lynda Carter) is an impossibly beautiful young woman who spends her days car–hopping at the local small–town burger joint, escaping the boredom of her surroundings with daydreams of making it big as a country music star. Into her life drives Lyle Wheeler (Marjoe), a smooth-talking young hustler and thief in a stolen car with a quick hand on the draw and an instant eye on Bobbie Jo, who doesn't take too much persuasion from Lyle to hop into his hot wheels and say goodbye to the stifling home life she shares with her alcoholic, religious momma Hattie (Peggy Stewart). Cruising around town and comparing their idols (Bobbie Jo's is Linda Ronstadt, while Lyle looks up to Billy the Kid because "he didn't take no shit from nobody"), the pair quickly form a bond over country music and soon find themselves alone out in the American desert, Bobbie Jo strumming an acoustic guitar and singing one of her compositions to Lyle. Smitten, Bobbie Jo and Lyle make love that evening, under the stars by firelight.

Welcoming the unexpected excitement entering her life with complete disregard for the potential consequences, Lyle is soon teaching Bobbie Jo how to handle a six-shooter and taking money from unhappy locals by using a handheld magnet to cheat at pinball competitions (a grift you could have pictured Marjoe himself utilizing in his time on the Santa Cruz boardwalk). With Bobbie Jo's hippy-esque girlfriend Essie Beaumont (Belinda Balaski) in tow, the trio drift aimlessly across the landscape, tripping on mushrooms and skinny-dipping in hot mud pools with Native Americans, Lyle hallucinating himself a life like "the good old days" in the Wild West. Lyle's fantasy soon becomes a reality after a town cop becomes suspicious of his hot wheels, and after a brief chase our outlaw anti-heroes are heading for a nearby town to seek refuge with Bobbie Jo's older sister Pearl (Merrie Lynn Ross), who works as a topless dancer in a local honky tonk dive bar.

Unfortunately, getting mixed-up with Pearl only makes things go from bad to worse for Lyle and Bobbie Jo, as Pearl's boyfriend Slick Callahan (Jesse Vint) quickly gets Lyle embroiled in a robbery in which a security guard is shot dead. Holed-up in a low-rent trailer park, Essie's attempt to resolve the situation peacefully ends in violence when she is shot dead by Sheriff Hicks (Gene Drew) and his men during a nighttime confrontation. Swearing vengeance over Essie's makeshift grade, Lyle cooks up a plan to humiliate the sheriff by robbing the local bank. They start by stealing M16 rifles and other weaponry from a gun and ammunition store, an angered Bobbie Jo now tearing up Main Street (and a couple of bodies) with bullets like a woman possessed ("I made them dance, didn't I?", she asks a surprised Lyle). When it comes time to mount the robbery, they do it in certain style, driving a pick-up truck through the window of the bank and dragging the large vault out onto the road with a chain, tearing off up the road as the heavy metal shoots up sparks as it is pulled along the asphalt.

Now with the law well and truly on their tail and their misadventures splashed across the tabloids ("New Youth Crime Spree" screams the heading above the photo of Lyle on the front cover of the *Southwest Enquirer*), our quartet of outlaws have to survive encounters with local deputies and heroic townsfolk out for a share of the reward, not to mention a rival quick draw artist named Joe Grant (Virgil Frye) who recognizes Lyle from the papers and places a bet against his talents, a bet he loses and pays for with his life. With a growing trail of bodies left behind them, and making no real attempt to stay hidden or go underground, it doesn't take long for Sheriff Hicks to corner Lyle, Bobbie Jo, Slick and Pearl, who have holed-up inside an old roadside curio store. In the ensuing shoot out, all but Bobbie Jo are shot dead, and the film ends with Bobbie Jo, in cuffs and standing over the bodies of Lyle and Slick, scowling and spitting at Sheriff Hicks as he reads a passage by Emmett Dalton that had been marked in a book on Western outlaws that Lyle carried around with him:

"The biggest fool on Earth is the one who thinks he can beat the law. That crime can be made to pay. It never paid, and never will. And that was the lesson of the Coffeyville raid." – Emmett Dalton (American outlaw).

Thanks in large part to the sturdy guidance of Mark L. Lester, *Bobbie Jo and the Outlaw* is a movie steeped in Americana, where the laws of the Wild West and outlaws like Bonnie and Clyde are as apple pie as anything else. Bobbie Jo and Lyle are both hopeless dreamers and romantics at heart, raised as much by gangster movies and late–night country radio as by actual parents or authority figures. Marjoe Gortner really brings a boyish, cocksure confidence to Lyle that helps explain why such a breathtakingly beautiful woman like Bobbie Jo would willingly throw her life away for him. Of course, unlike his heroes, Lyle is not really a gangster, he just takes his worship of them a little too far, and is not really equipped to deal with the consequences of playing in that outlaw world.

Interestingly, according to Lester (in an interview featurette on the Blu–ray release of the film), Marjoe and his manager initially demanded a $10,000 payday to take the role in the film, a figure which the filmmakers baulked at as being well above the usual figure that an actor of Gortner's stature would command for such a production. Lester advised Marjoe's manager that unless his client had signed the contract for the originally offered (and undisclosed) amount by 5pm on the deadline date, then the role would be offered to Lester's back–up choice for the male lead: Sylvester Stallone. By 5pm, the contract had been signed, saving *Bobbie Jo and the Outlaw* from becoming the very different film it likely would have been with a young Sly Stallone playing Lyle Wheeler.

A moderate hit on the drive–in circuit upon its original release, *Bobbie Jo and the Outlaw* may have quickly faded from public memory, like so many others of its type, were it not for the presence of Lynda Carter in the role of Bobbie Jo. A former Miss World America (1972), Carter was a virtual unknown as an acting entity when she made her film debut in *Bobbie Jo and the Outlaw* after a couple of TV guest roles in shows like *Matt Helm* (1975–1976) and *Starsky and Hutch*. On April the 21st 1976, less than a month after *Bobbie Jo and the Outlaw* opened, the first episode of *Wonder Woman* (1975–1979) debuted on ABC with Lynda Carter in the title role. Though Carter had first played Wonder Woman (and her alter–ego Diana Prince) in a pilot movie that aired in November of 1975, it was the success of the series which quickly helped catapult her to stardom. Playing the sexy superhero with the golden lasso and star–spangled outfit brought Lynda Carter an enduring status as an icon of 1970s pop–culture, and the star was able to use the initial success of *Wonder Woman* to land lucrative modelling and cosmetic contracts, soda commercials and a best–selling poster, not to mention record albums and television specials. Naturally, when *Wonder Woman* started racing up the Nielsen charts, distributors were keen to put *Bobbie Jo and the Outlaw* back on the drive–in screens to cash–in on the show's success. Carter, at the time an outspoken born–again Christian, refused to help promote or to even discuss the film, in which she appeared topless in several scenes, and did her best to ensure it could not be seen. The ensuing years saw *Bobbie Jo and the Outlaw* become something of a minor cult film, primarily on the back of Carter's appearance, and frame blow-ups of her nude scenes became a frequent inclusion in many of those *Celebrity Skin*–type magazines that were published in the 1980s.

Belinda Balaski on Marjoe Gortner

Born in Inglewood, California, Belinda Balaski is an actress, writer, artist and photographer who attracted a cult audience through her work with director Joe Dante, appearing in movies like *Piranha* (1978), *The Howling* (1981), *Gremlins* (1984), its sequel *Gremlins: The Next Batch* (1989) and *Matinee* (1990). She also worked on a number of classic episodic television shows including *Baretta* (1975–1978), *S.W.A.T.* (1975–1976), *Starsky & Hutch*, *Charlie's Angels* (1976–1981), *Vega$* (1978–1981) and *Hunter* (1984–1991), as well as a slew of TV Movies of the Week and After School Specials. Belinda co-starred alongside Marjoe in *Bobbie Jo and the Outlaw* and *Food of the Gods*.

When was the first time you heard you were going to be working with Marjoe, in Bobbie Jo and the Outlaw? Had you heard or been aware of Marjoe prior?

Such an interesting question, especially for me. I had heard of Marjoe multiple times before I worked with him. I lived up in the Half Moon Bay area back in 1968–69. It was a small community in northern California where my ex and I had a restaurant on the coast, and there was quite a bit of rumor about the mother of Marjoe Gortner, who lived somewhere in town. There were so many stories about these things she had done to her son to make him learn his speeches as a child evangelist of four–years–old that were not good, and a lot of the people in town viewed her as an evil woman, and would tiptoe around her property, never knocking on her door. They avoided her at all cost. That was the first time I became aware of Marjoe Gortner.

Then I came to L.A. around November of 1970, and in 1974 was cast in a Jack Arnold film called *Black Eye* (1974), which was actually a pilot movie for a proposed Fred Williamson TV series. I was cast as an evangelistic convert who goes into one of those deliriums when she is touched on the forehead. So for the audition I rented Marjoe's self-exposing documentary, which I had seen in 1972, to research this character and how to be this character and fall into a feverish religious frenzy. I watched that documentary multiple times so I could get this part in *Black Eye*, and of course I did end up landing the role, so that was my second introduction to Marjoe (actually the third, if you count discovering the magnificent documentary in the first place).

Then a couple of years later, I was in a film workshop with acting teacher Lieux Dressler, which Mary Lynn Ross was also in, and Lynda Carter and Peggy Stewart were also studying. Mary Lynn's boyfriend at the time, Mark Lester, was putting this film together and came in to watch several of us showcase some scene work. I was doing theatre as well as the workshop, going back and forth and Peggy Stewart was playing my mother in a play called *Picnic* with Nick Nolte. Well Mark ended up casting Peggy as Lynda Carter's mother in *Bobbie Jo and the Outlaw* and I was cast as Lynda's best friend Essie, and of course Mary Lynn played that wonderful "fluffy floozie" as I liked to call her, with Marjoe as our lead guy. It really was rather phenomenal, because that was 1976 and almost ten years of knowing and virtually studying this person, then finally meeting and working with him.

WILDCAT!

Bobbie Jo (Lynda Carter), Essie Beaumont (Belinda Balaski) and Lyle Wheeler (Marjoe Gortner) find time for a bit of fun while on the lam. American lobby card for *Bobbie Jo and the Outlaw*.

Your introduction to Marjoe makes an interesting contrast to what many others who worked with him have said, that they had no idea about Marjoe's past, and usually didn't find out until after the film was released or maybe half-way through a shoot if word had gotten around.
I was *so* aware of his background going in, I probably knew as much about him as he knew about himself! And he and I became really good friends. But Marjoe is not one to "bank upon his past." He's more an "ever present and in the moment" type of guy!

It was a really nice characterization you came up with in Bobbie Jo, she had a bit of the late–60s flower child hangover about her with the round granny glasses and her anti–violence stance, which puts her at interesting odds with the people and situations happening around her. Well you know, I thought here I am going to be on film playing Lynda Carter's best friend, so I called Mark Lester up after meeting with her and I said "Look, I want to dye my hair red, have these special beveled glasses made and gain about thirty pounds, because best friends are often opposites and I can't compete with Lynda on camera, she's way too beautiful. I'd rather go character." Mark said he loved the red hair, he loved the glasses, but he didn't want me to gain a pound! So that was my compromise. I decided to go "character" because it would be so much fun and so much more believable as her best friend.

When you watch Lynda Carter in the Blu–ray of Bobbie Jo and the Outlaw, she almost looks like some CGI creation, she seems so flawless, statuesque and doll–like, just an amazing visual screen presence. She is actually perfect! And her voice is perfect as well, her singing voice. And the interesting thing is that my boyfriend at the time was a musician named J. C. Crowley, who wrote a song called "Baby Come Back" the night we broke up, which became a big hit in 1977 for his band Player. But before he wrote that song, when we were still together, I was on the set of *Bobbie Jo and the Outlaw* and overheard Mark saying that he needed to come up with a song for Lynda to sing in the film, for the scene where she and Marjoe were out in the desert. So I told Mark about J.C. and the beautiful songs he has written and Mark said, "Where is he?" Now at that time we were shooting in New Mexico and J.C. was back in L.A. So sure enough, once I called J.C. and told him about the opportunity he drove straight to New Mexico to meet with Mark and played a song for him in his motel room and Mark loved it, so he taught it to Lynda Carter and she sings it to Marjoe in the film. He also wrote that great opening theme song to *Bobbie Jo & the Outlaw* ("Those City Lights") with another old friend Chick Rains, which was performed by Bobby Bare.

How did you find Marjoe the first time you actually met him, after being aware of him for so long via the documentary and living not far from his mother some years earlier and hearing all the rumors about his childhood? Did he seem like the person you would have imagined someone to be with that sort of background and upbringing?

Marjoe is a force (laughs). He is not a person, he's a force that you have to reckon with. He arrives on the set not at 100% but at 500%, and he remains at that level even when he starts at five am and works a fifteen–hour day on set! After that fifteen hours he will then invite everyone back to his guest house on location and cook them dinner, mind you he's doing all the cooking himself, *and* he's still going long after dinner entertaining everyone! He has the most amazing energy of anyone I've ever met.

You can get that sense from the documentary. He seems to channel this great energy that doesn't let up, either on stage or off.

I have such great respect for that man. He is amazing. He is truly an amazing human being.

And you obviously connected well on set, considering the chemistry you generate together on screen.

I think he has issues with women, and I think it was hard for Lynda to work with him because of that, so in a way I was kind of the safe ground between them. I became good friends with Lynda and I became good friends with Marjoe. Because I was easy to be friends with, particularly playing the character I did in that movie, who was no real sexual threat to the relationship between Marjoe and Lynda's characters. We gelled easily, and the next thing I knew I was being called into the offices at AIP (American International Pictures) for a follow–up movie.

Marjoe already had a two–picture deal with AIP, for *Bobbie Jo* and *Food of the Gods*. At the time I didn't know that at all, but at the end of filming *Bobbie Jo* AIP called me in and told me they wanted me for this other film they were doing. So I decided to go in a completely different direction with the character I was cast as in *Food of the Gods*.

The pregnant young lady who was trapped with her boyfriend in their camper van that had broken down on the side of the road. And there was a little bit of women's lib and independence about that character you played, because she was pregnant but didn't feel like she needed to be married to her partner, even though he was keen to tie the knot and make the relationship "official."

Yes, exactly, that's right.

And just briefly going back to Bobbie Jo, your character of Essie was interesting because there was an element of resentment towards her from Marjoe's character, who feels like you are getting in the middle of his relationship with Bobbie Jo, and also your character was very much the peaceful one of the group, who really spoke out against violence, and of course she is the first one of them to be killed, when she is shot by the police during the confrontation at the trailer park, which I thought added a nice touch of irony to the screenplay.

Yeah she was definitely a "third wheel" character with a nice death scene. And I was really nervous filming it, because they only had one pair of blue and white striped overalls, and I had never worked with squibs to simulate bullet hits before! So they decided to film it with five cameras live at different angles just in case, because we only had the one chance to get it right and those overalls would be unusable after that. I was super nervous because I had never done a death scene before, or worked with blood effects, so I was just really worried about doing it right. But it was great fun, I ended up doing it perfectly and it was really great fun to do.

I love that film, I really do. It has its issues, but it has a cast of amazing actors and I think that was due to the genius of Mark Lester and Mary Lynne Ross, they knew how to assemble a cast that would not only really gel together, but would also pitch-in and work hard to make a low-budget film that would really come off successfully. I mean there's Jim Gammon, Virgil Frye, Jesse Vint, Gerrit Graham, Gene Drew. I think there was a lot of heart and soul put in that film, and it shows in the finished result.

Interestingly, Mark Lester has said that his second choice for the male lead, if Marjoe didn't sign the contract offered to him by the due date, was Sylvester Stallone, which would have resulted in quite a different film I would imagine!

Yes, and quite a difference in height between Lynda and Sylvester!

How did Marjoe and Lynda get along? At the time of filming she would have been right on the verge of superstardom, thanks to her role on TV as Wonder Woman.

It was difficult for him to get along with a lot of women, I think due to the issues with his mother and Lynda is all woman, you know. Wonder Woman. And I think that that was an uncomfortable confront for him. I think he likes to be in control, not being controlled, and I think he was in a situation for most of his early life where he was being controlled, and I don't think he likes to lose that control. I don't want to try and be overly psychoanalytical about it, but that was kind of the way I saw it from my perspective.

I guess when you look at his past and how he was treated and controlled and taken advantage of, you can understand how he would have developed some trust issues after he grew up and was on his own.

And then he hit a point where he didn't trust himself. That's why he made the documentary. He knew that preaching was something he could always fall back on and make a lot of money doing, if he had to. But he didn't want to do that anymore and he didn't want to be tempted by it, so he exposed himself in the documentary in order to take away any future temptation. And that's the very essence of Marjoe that I love so much.

The doco was almost like a cleansing of his soul and conscience, as well as an emphatic full-stop to and virtual self-sabotaging of his preaching lifestyle.

That's exactly right. Which was absolutely brilliant of him, and showed his true depth of character.

When you watch him on-screen in movies like Bobbie Jo and the Outlaw and Food of the Gods, you can see the charisma that he generated on stage in revival houses show through in his performances and in the manic energy he brings to his acting.

I tell you, he's a hard man to take your eyes off of. When there's a vast amount of people around, the person you find yourself looking at is Marjoe, he just pulls focus.

Bobbie Jo of course became notorious as the only film in which Lynda Carter appeared nude, having shot a topless sex scene with Marjoe and also skinny-dipping with him and yourself in the scene where you eat magic mushrooms with the older Native American and trip together in a hot mud springs out in the desert.

It was supposed to be a natural hot spring in the script! However we had to pretend it was relaxing and warm, but in reality, we were all freezing and shivering in there! Oh my gosh, it was so cold, but then again I guess that's why it's called "acting"!

It wasn't long after Bobbie Jo that Carter found her big fame on TV as Wonder Woman, but also became a rather strong born again Christian, which caused her to turn her back on the movie and pretty much ignore it or refuse to speak about it, primarily because of the publicity it generated due to her topless scenes.

I think once she became very Christian, around the time of *Wonder Woman*, she started looking at changing up a lot of things that hadn't been working in her life, and began devoting a lot of herself to God and was just very upset that she had ever exposed herself in that way on camera. And she tried to get Mark to cut her nude scenes out of the film, it became kind of a war, I don't know how things specifically went down regarding that, but I know she tried really hard to have those scenes removed.

Any interesting stories or memories from the filming of Food of the Gods for Bert I. Gordon?

Oh yes, most definitely. We went to Bowen Island off Vancouver for *Food of the Gods*, and Bert had chosen this location because of its grey, foggy atmosphere. So we get up there and shoot maybe three or four days of exteriors and everything is really grey and foggy and perfect, and the next day we woke–up and it had snowed, and everything was white! Then it continued to snow. And Bert's face is getting worse and worse, you can see him thinking "Oh my God", because his entire exterior is now white, it's no longer gray and dull and foggy. And the trees are white and none of it matches what we had already shot the week before. It was costing Bert so much money and we ended up having to stay there a lot longer than planned.

And on top of that, here's Ida Lupino, who is not really enjoying being stuck on this itty bitty island, and she's hiking around the island at four o'clock in the morning going completely crazy, because there weren't any clubs or cafes or any place to go, and we're all stuck in the little places we were staying at. We would have dinner together, and Ralph Meeker would play piano and Ida would sit on top of the baby grand and sing. Oh how I wish I had had my home movie camera with me at the time. Then after dinner, everybody would retreat to their rooms or cottages, but Ida would continue to "haunt the hallway"!!! After about the first week Ida approached Bert one morning around 5am and said "Bert, I've written my own death scene, and if you don't shoot it, I'm leaving anyway." (Laughs). Bert looked shocked and said "What are you talking about? Your character is the only one who lives through the whole movie!" And Ida just shot back "Well, I'm leaving on the four o'clock ferry today, so you better do some rewriting and shoot my death scene." And she did! She was on that four o'clock ferry when it pulled away from the island.

Oh and here's another story. I remember Bert telling me to scream in the final scene up on the balcony whenever I saw the big giant rat and I finally said "Bert, I'm not going to scream anymore, OK? I've been screaming for three weeks and it will become ineffective." Bert said "This is the big scream at the climax of the movie" and I told him "No. It would be more effective if I opened my mouth and tried to scream but no sound came out." which is exactly what I did in several succeeding takes and he kept yelling "CUT!" I need you to scream, and then he'd call "action" & I wouldn't scream again and he got so mad he finally yelled "That's LUNCH!" at about 7am and stomped off screaming "I could have hired Fay Wray!." Omg are you kidding! My entire soundtrack on that film if you looped it together sounds like multiple orgasms! I'm either running from rats, breathing heavily, having a baby or screaming!!!

Did you get the sense that Marjoe was happy working on these lower-budgeted, more drive-in oriented action and horror films?
I think on these films he felt like he had more control, as opposed to working at Universal in bigger-budgeted films like *Earthquake*. Even on *When You Comin' Back, Red Ryder* I'm sure he had more control as well, because he was also a producer on that one. But he is not someone who follows other peoples' direction too well. He's going to try and have it his own way, and actually that's what I liked about him. His inner strength and instincts are amazing. He might not be the most brilliant actor in the world but that guy's intentions are always spot on. Nobody ever tried harder or worked harder on set, he always gave at least 500%.

Even seeing Food of the Gods for the first time as a twelve-year-old, having no idea who Marjoe Gortner was, just his natural screen presence and charisma leaped out at me and created such an impact that he became someone I instantly gravitated towards whenever I spotted him in anything else.
Mm-hmm, I agree, he really is quite something.

Did you stay in touch with him after you made the two movies together at AIP?
Well for a while we did, yes. But then I moved to Hawaii and he went off into his relationships and other movies, and by the time I came back everyone had kind of moved on. And then some years back I started to appear at these fan conventions, and everybody was wanting to find him. Everybody wanted him to appear at these shows, but I don't know, I don't think he really wants to be found.

As much as you would love to see him out there meeting with fans, the fact that he does keep such a low profile helps add to the enigma of Marjoe.
Well you know, he has certainly earned his right to privacy. He has been a public figure since he was four–years–old, so he has the right to choose that anonymity for himself. I miss him and would love to see him again sometime, but I do honor and respect the fact that he seems to want his privacy. There's nothing wrong with that, when you have given so much of yourself to living a public life, at some point you are bound to say, "That's enough."

ACAPULCO GOLD
USA/June 1, 1976/88 minutes
Director: Burt Brinckerhoff
Writers: Don Enright & O'Brian Tomalin
Producers: Allan F. Bodoh & Bruce Cohn
Cast: Marjoe Gortner, Robert Lansing, Ed Nelson, John Harkins & Randi Oakes
AKA: The Heroin Connection

In the 1970s, the life of a big–time drug runner began to have an air of exotic excitement and prestige about it, at least amongst some circles of society. People who had been through the widespread infiltration of marijuana into suburban American homes which began in the mid–sixties and later experimented with LSD (a Lovely Sort of Death), then saw the demand for heroin go through the roof as idealistic young sixties hippies became burned–out, discarded junkies. The late–seventies brought in another seismic shift, as cocaine became the drug of choice for the disco and Studio 54 crowds, and businessmen wanting to get the most for themselves out of the so–called 'Me Decade'.

Set amongst the backdrop of the South American drug trade,

Acapulco Gold is a strange though sadly quite unexciting crime adventure. Though the title is clearly inspired by the popular and potent strain of cannabis that was first discovered in the early–sixties, the story actually revolves around heroin and real gold of the 14–carat variety. Marijuana still does have a presence in the film, however, as we first meet smiling American tourist Ralph Hollio (Marjoe Gortner) in the back of a Mexican taxi as it makes its way to the airport. "Something to remember Mehico", the driver proclaims as he offers a toke of his fat joint to Ralph as he rides in the backseat. "Mucho grass-ias", Ralph jokes before taking a long toke then adding "When they legalize this stuff, I'm still going to enjoy it."

An insurance salesman with a passion for yachting, when Ralph arrives at the airport for his flight back to the United States, a nun carrying a piñata in the shape of a dog approaches and tells him that she would love to swap her piñata for the one which he is carrying, which is in the shape of a chicken. The bemused Ralph agrees to the swap before the nun quickly realizes that she has made a mistake and swapped piñatas with the wrong man. As a team of cops pounce on the confused American, a gunfight breaks out inside the airport, causing chaos and resulting in the death of the nun. When Ralph is taken into custody and the chicken piñata broken open, it is revealed to contain packages of pure heroin. His protests of innocence falling on deaf ears, Ralph is thrown into a jail cell and is soon joined by Carl Solborg (Robert Lansing), a one-time America's Cup winner now a boozed–up shell of his former self, hiring himself out as a captain for any dubious job that might come along.

It isn't long before Carl is bailed out by Morgan (John Harkins), a balding, middle–aged crook who wants to hire him to sail a yacht from Acapulco to Hawaii in 21 days. Suspicious about the job, Carl eventually accepts the offer but decides he could use Ralph's sailing knowledge and company on the trip, and finds it easy to break his fellow American out of his jail cell by plying the guard with cheap booze and even cheaper hookers. It isn't long before Ralph is free and shirtless and enjoying the sun aboard Morgan's yacht, unaware that the cargo they are transporting is not drugs as suspected, but gold, which has been carefully hidden as part of the boat's ballast. Once the gold is safely in Hawaii, Morgan plans to trade it with a Chinaman named Mr. Wang for twenty–million–dollars–worth of high–grade heroin, which has been ingeniously hidden inside a shipment of golf balls! It all climaxes with a somewhat comical chase across a golf course, as Carl reveals himself to be an undercover agent, Ralph falls in love with Sally Cantrell (Randi Oakes), Morgan's young blonde companion/assistant, and the trio sail off into the sunset as new best buddies with grand plans to start up their own charter boat business.

Acapulco Gold can't decide if it wants to be a straight adventure story or a stoner comedy. Ultimately, it doesn't work very well as either, and it's no surprise that the film was quickly relegated to obscurity in most territories (though it was dusted off and put–on as the support feature to Cheech & Chong's *Up in Smoke* when it played Los Angeles in 1978). The attempts at humor in the film fall pretty flat—moments like the loud (and loudly–dressed) middle–aged tourists who have their fishing boat hijacked by the heroin dealers, and later show up again on the golf course during the climactic chase (in fact it is the obnoxious male tourist who inadvertently helps wrap–up the case by hitting Mr. Wang on the head with a stray golf ball, knocking him unconscious and sending him over a cliff in his out–of–control golf cart). The attempts at humorous dialogue are also rather groan-inducing ("Oh, you enforce the taking of drugs?", one man enquires when introduced to a member of the Drug Enforcement Agency).

Sally Cantrell (Randi Oakes) and Ralph Hollio (Marjoe Gortner) enjoy a moment of calm on the seas in *Acapulco Gold*.

Another area where *Acapulco Gold* falls flat is in its disappointing cinematography by Robert Steadman, a usually reliable lensman who had photographed the gritty *Hammer* (1972) with Fred Williamson, as well as providing underwater and second unit work on the Bond movie *Never Say Never Again* (1983) and Robert Zemeckis' horror thriller *What Lies Beneath* (2000). Unfortunately, his work on *Acapulco Gold* has for the most part a bland TV look to it, and doesn't use the potential offered by such exotic and scenic locales, though there is one truly breathtaking sequence, where a helicopter takes a dizzying low–level flight along a stretch of the Hawaiian coast, which almost compensates for the visual dullness of the rest of the movie.

Highlighted by Marjoe, who does manage to inject a boyish, likeable quality into his character and performs his limited material quite well, it's the cast assembled for *Acapulco Gold* which help the film retain some interest, particularly for those with a love of 1970s American television. Randi Oakes, making one of her first acting appearances here, would go on to establish herself as something of a television sex symbol, thanks to her classic blonde look and appearances in shows like *Fantasy Island*, *The Love Boat* (1977–1987), *Battlestar Galactica* (1978–1979) and, most predominately, *CHiPS* (1977–1983), in which she appeared as Officer Bonnie Clark for 66 episodes. Her career slowed down after she married actor Gregory Harrison in 1980 (the pair had met the year before on the *Battle of the Network Stars VII* TV special), and she pretty much retired from acting in 1985. Ed Nelson, who plays DEA agent Ray Hollister in the film, also had an extensive list of episodic television to his credit, dating back to the late–fifties, and also appeared in a slew of great 1950s B–movies like *Swamp Women* (1956), *Attack of the Crab Monsters* (1957), *Invasion of the Saucer Men* (1957), *A Bucket of Blood* (1959) and others, while later film roles included *Airport '75* and *Midway*. Tall and with tough, ruggedly handsome looks, Robert Lansing was another familiar television face, who also had roles in the offbeat sci-fi film *4D Man* (1959), Bert I. Gordon's *Empire of the Ants* (1977) and the enjoyably tacky creature features *Island Claws* (1980) and *The Nest* (1988).

Director Burt Brinckerhoff forged his career primarily on television, helming episodes of *Baretta*, *Dynasty*, *Lou Grant* (1977–1982), *Hart to Hart* (1979–1984), *After M*A*S*H* (1983–1985), *Moonlighting* (1985–1989), *Remington Steele* (1982–1987), *Magnum P.I.* (1980–1988), *ALF* (1986–1990) and many others. He also directed the canine carnage horror movie *Dogs* (1976), though his best work was perhaps the 1974 telemovie *The Invasion of Carol Enders*, a supernatural thriller starring Meredith Baxter and produced by the famous Dan Curtis (who reportedly ghost-directed a lot of the movie also).

THE FOOD OF THE GODS
USA/June 18, 1976/88 minutes
Director: Bert I. Gordon
Writer: Bert I. Gordon
Producer: Samuel Z. Arkoff & Bert I. Gordon
Cast: Marjoe Gortner, Pamela Franklin, Ralph Meeker, Belinda Balaski, Jon Cypher, John McLiam & Ida Lupino

Portrait of Marjoe Gortner as Morgan in *The Food of the Gods*.

In the late–1950s, Wisconsin–born filmmaker Bert I. Gordon established himself as the director, screenwriter and special effects artist on a number of low–budget, black & white horror movies produced by American International Pictures (AIP), which proved to be popular with the young drive–in audience and rabid kids who began devouring Forry Ackerman's *Famous Monsters of Filmland* when it began publishing in 1958. Gigantism was a popular and continual theme that ran throughout many of Gordon's hits such as *The Amazing Colossal Man* (1957) and its pseudo–sequel *War of the Colossal Beast* (1958), as well as *The Cyclops* (1957), *Beginning of the End* (1957) and *Earth vs. the Spider* (1958). Gordon's fascination with all things oversized earned him the endearing nickname of "Mister B.I.G" amongst his fans (although he did on occasion take size to the other extreme, such as in 1958's *Attack of the Puppet People*).

Gordon had previously used the 1904 H. G. Wells speculative fiction novel *The Food of the Gods and How It Came to Earth* as the (very loose) inspiration for his absurd, but lots of fun, fantasy film *Village of the Giants* (1965), in which a bunch of rebellious and raucous teenagers (led by Beau Bridges) take over a small town after ingesting a mysterious substance called "Goo" and grow to giant size. Also featuring Johnny Crawford swinging from Joy Harmon's giant boobs, an appearance by The Beau Brummels and a very young Ron Howard (as the boy genius who invents the substance that causes the gigantism), *Village of the Giants* captured a lot of the same ambience as the series of *Beach Party* films which were popular at the time, and although not a huge success upon its initial release it has since gone on to become a cult camp favorite.

A decade after *Village of the Giants*, Mister B.I.G. returned to the Wells novel to helm yet another adaptation, this time keeping the title but shortening it to simply *The Food of the Gods* and adding a disclaimer at the start of the film that it was only "loosely based on a portion" of the novel. That's covering yourself. Gordon's *The Food of the Gods* casts Marjoe Gortner as Morgan, a professional football player who takes the ferry over to an island in British Columbia to get some rest and relaxation before the upcoming big game.

"One of these days the Earth will get even with Man for messing her up with his garbage", Morgan muses to himself in voice-over, recalling his father's prediction as the ferry approaches the picturesque island. Unfortunately, an idyllic weekend soon turns into a nightmare as Morgan's travelling companion and teammate Davis (Chuck Courtney) is attacked and killed by a giant wasp after riding his horse into the woods to chase a deer. When Morgan discovers his buddy dead, his face horribly swollen by a huge dose of venom, he races off to a nearby cabin in search of some help, only to be confronted in the barn by a giant rooster and a brood of oversized chickens! Amazingly, after fighting off the aggressive rooster and killing it with a pitchfork, Morgan remains remarkably unfazed by the whole experience, storming up to the cabin and shouting "Where the hell did you get those goddam chickens?!?" to the middle-aged lady watching him through the kitchen window.

It turns out that the occupant of the cabin, Mr. Skinner (John McLiam) and his wife (Ida Lupino) have been feeding their livestock with a mysterious thick white liquid which has started coming up through a hole in the ground outside their cabin, a mysterious substance that the Skinners hope will make them rich and solve the world's hunger problems but just ends up causing more terror after a plague of rats ingest this gift from God and, after growing to the size of a motorbike, scurrying across the countryside and terrorizing not only Morgan and the Skinners but stranded young couple Thomas and Rita (Tom Stovall and Belinda Balaski), greedy dog food manufacturer Jack Bensington (Ralph Meeker) who wants exclusive rights to market the miraculous but deadly substance, and his young assistant Lorna (Pamela Franklin), a bacteriologists brought along to analyze the Food of the Gods.

Morgan (Marjoe Gortner) arrives too late to save his buddy Davis (Chuck Courtney) from the deadly sting of a gigantic wasp in *The Food of the Gods.*

In his second attempt at transferring Wells' novel to the screen, Bert I. Gordon turns *The Food of the Gods* into another entry in the Nature Strikes Back sub–genre of horror cinema which experienced a period of popularity in the seventies, as evidenced in films like *Frogs* (1972), *Night of the Lepus* (1972) and *Day of the Animals* (1977).

Marjoe's character in *The Food of the Gods* is interesting. On one hand, Morgan is very much the confident, sporty outdoorsman that you would love to have in your corner in times of crises, when courage and a cool head are required. Yet at other times, he comes across as both selfish and pig–headed, and his actions and determination to see things done his way ultimately leads to the death of his friend Brian (Jon Cypher), whom Morgan has not only dragged back to the island at his reluctance but insists upon him riding shotgun in his open–top jeep despite the obvious dangers from the giant wasps and rats around them.

Morgan is also depicted as very much an Alpha–male of the time, and Marjoe exudes all the associated qualities quite effectively here. Within moments of meeting Morgan, the young Lorna thinks she has him all worked out:

"You don't like women around when you are doing your thing, do you?"

"What's my thing?"

"Facing danger."

Later, as the cabin is being surrounded by an army of hungry giant rats and survival is looking less likely, the bookish and somewhat nerdy, short–haired Lorna admits to Morgan that she wants him to make love to her in the middle of all this craziness, a request which Morgan takes in his stride and promises to follow up on once he saves the day (which he eventually does by fashioning a couple of pipe bombs and blowing the wall on a nearby dam, flooding the immediate area and drowning all the rats).

Though the central story of *The Food of the Gods* wraps everything up rather neatly, it tacks on a bleak epilogue in which some of the mysterious nutrient is swept upstream in a river and ingested by cattle, who are then milked and the dairy shipped off to a grade school, where the infected product is drunk by a classroom of small kids, who will no doubt succumb to the same form of gigantism that affected all of the baby animal and insect life that came into contact with it (it is established in the film that the Food of the Gods only affects infants and not fully–developed lifeforms). The epilogue provides a nice little nod and tie to Bert I. Gordon's previous adaptation of the Wells' story, *Village of the Giants* (the original Wells novel also dealt with human gigantism).

Marketed with a luridly exciting poster painted by Drew Struzan (whose iconic film poster work includes the *Star Wars* and *Indiana Jones* series), *The Food of the Gods* turned out to be decent hit for AIP, raking in around one million dollars in America during its initial theatrical release (a very good figure for an AIP release at the time), and the film proved popular in a number of overseas markets (including Australia, where it was paired on a double–bill with Jeff Lieberman's *Squirm*, another—and quite excellent—AIP low–budget shocker from 1976). A sequel, *Food of the Gods II* (*aka Gnaw: Food of the Gods II*) was belatedly released in 1989, but it bared no connection to the original film and was produced by a completely different creative group.

A classic piece of Drew Struzan art highlights the original American one-sheet poster for *The Food of the Gods*.

MAYDAY AT 40,000 FEET!
USA/November 12, 1976/97 minutes
Director: Robert Butler
Writers: Austin Ferguson, Dick Nelson & Andrew J. Fenady
Producer: Andrew J. Fenady
Cast: David Janssen, Don Meredith, Christopher George, Ray Milland, Lynda Day George & Marjoe Gortner

A made for TV disaster film clearly inspired by the success of the first two *Airport* films, *Mayday at 40,000 Feet!* once again sees Marjoe cast in the roll of a sociopathic villain, playing here a tightly–wound criminal named Greco, who is behind bars in Salt Lake City and waiting to be escorted on a commercial flight back to New York to face a double murder charge. The drama aboard the Boeing 727 starts well before then, however, as Transcon Airways Flight 602 first takes off for its final destination from Los Angeles and is already brimming with an assortment of cliched disaster film characters with soap opera problems.

At the top of the passenger list is an aging Ray Milland as the loud and obnoxious Joseph Mannheim, a once–prominent doctor now disgraced by a malpractice suit taken out by an accident victim that he had raced to help. Broken by the experience and no longer trustful of people, Mannheim drowns out his bitterness and disappointment with a steady supply of scotch. Piloting the passenger airline are Captain Pete Douglas (David Janssen), First Officer Stan Burkhart (Christopher George) and Second Officer Mike Fuller (Don Meredith). While Burkhart and Fuller sit in the cockpit ogling the stewardesses and making innuendos about them being young enough to still have their "baby fat", Douglas is a lot more serious and sullen, his mind distracted by thoughts of his wife, who has had to take herself to hospital to have a biopsy taken on a lump she has discovered in her breast.

Sam Riese (Broderick Crawford) will not be able to keep Greco (Marjoe Gortner) in cuffs for much longer. *Mayday at 40,000 Feet!*

Also on board is Sam Riese (Broderick Crawford), a Federal Marshall assigned the task of escorting Greco on the flight and ensuring he gets to New York without incident. Not in the best physical shape, the way Riese gasps for breath and clutches at a discomfort in his left arm and chest, you just know a heart attack is on its way. It arrives not long after Greco is brought aboard in Salt Lake City. Having already staged an escape attempt while being transported from the prison to the airport (with eight pounds of lead strapped to his ankle), it's obvious that Greco is not going to go along quietly, and surprising that the authorities have left it up to one lone, out of shape and middle–aged male to keep this clearly unbalanced wildcat in line.

Once the flight is back up in the air, things settle down briefly, before Riese suddenly keels over in his seat and the handcuffed Greco, sensing his opportunity, retrieves a handgun from inside the dying man's coat. A rather brief scuttle ensues and Greco is quickly subdued, but not before he fires off a volley of wild shots, one of which hits a female passenger in the back, while another one injures Captain Douglas and another severs a vital hydraulic fluid line that helps control the airliner's wing flaps and landing gear.

With a major snowstorm keeping all nearby airports closed, the crippled jet and its injured occupants have to endure a three-hour flight to Chicago, the nearest airport that is open and big enough the handle the huge aircraft. The treacherous trip provides ample time for Mannheim to come out of his bitter alcoholic self-absorption and learn to help people who are in need again, while Burkhart and Fuller sweat it out in the cockpit, wondering just how much control over the plane the damaged hydraulics will let them have. A strong crosswind blowing across Chicago makes landing the airliner even more precarious, though when the moment comes the 727 touches down with little more than a few rough bounces. The chaos of the landing gives Greco another chance to make an escape, but he is quickly stopped by Burkhart. Things tie themselves up neatly with a final scene at the hospital, where we find out that the injured passengers will survive and the lump found in the breast of the Captain's wife is a benign tumor.

It's unfortunate that Marjoe was not given a bit more to do in *Mayday at 40,000 Feet!*, as he is quite good and effective in the rather limited screen time he is given (one of the drawbacks of the big 1970s disaster film genre is they were so packed with characters it made it a bit restrictive to try and explore each one in any kind of depth, especially in a telemovie like this, which ran about an hour shorter than the standard Irwin Allen epic). Gortner plays Greco as a cocky, slimy hood with a boyish exterior. "He sure looks like a cutie", Federal Marshall Riese observes when he is shown a photograph of Greco, who we first meet in a Salt Lake prison, throwing his food around the cell and attacking an inmate who dares to taunt him about what fate may await the double murderer once he arrives in New York. "They have to get me there first", he seethes with a look of crazed determination in his eyes. Once aboard the flight to New York, Greco repulses one of the stewardesses by kissing her on the neck as she walks past him, a great touch by Marjoe that brings an even sleazier aspect to his already rotten character. Surprisingly, even the contentious 'N' word is uttered by Gortner here, as Greco talks down to a black American serviceman passenger who has been charged with keeping an eye on the prisoner after Riese suffers his fatal heart attack.

Based on the 1973 novel *Jetstream* by Austin Ferguson, *Mayday at 40,000 Feet!* is given solid if pedestrian TV movie direction by two-time Emmy winner Robert Butler, a veteran of many classic small screen television shows including *The Twilight Zone* (1959–1964), *Batman* (1966–1968), *Star Trek* (1966–1969) and, later in his career, *Hill Street Blues* (1981–1987), *Moonlighting* and *Lois and Clark: The New Adventures of Superman* (1993–1997). Feature film wise, he helmed the classic Kurt Russell Disney comedy *The Computer Wore Tennis Shoes* (1967) and the teen sex comedy *Up the Creek* (1984). In the nineties, he returned to the air disaster genre with *Turbulence* (1997), a film which bared some definite thematic similarities to *Mayday at 40,000 Feet!* (in *Turbulence*, Ray Liotta plays an incarcerated serial killer who causes havoc aboard a 747 while flying from New York to L.A. to stand trial).

VIVA KNIEVEL!
USA/June 1977/106 minutes
Director: Gordon Douglas
Writers: Antonio Santean (as Antonio Santillan) & Norman Katkov
Producer: Stanley Hough
Cast: Evel Knievel, Gene Kelly, Lauren Hutton, Red Buttons, Leslie Nielsen, Cameron Mitchell, Frank Gifford, Dabney Coleman & Marjoe Gortner

While his legend was effectively born with his famous jump over the fountains at Caesar's Palace in Las Vegas on December 31, 1967, daredevil motorcyclist Evel Knievel was a true icon of the American 1970s, embodying so many of the traits which we associate with the 'Me Decade'. Brash, full of bravado, arrogance and self-confidence, with a wild side and a taste for hard liquor, expensive boys toys and a visual flamboyance that made him the Elvis Presley of the daredevil set. Performing his death-defying leaps over rows of cars and buses to sold-out stadium audiences across America (along with one memorable jump at London's Wembley Stadium), Knievel tapped into a zeitgeist of the times and became a cultural phenomenon, particularly popular amongst boys in their pre and early-teens. Knievel became a one-man corporation that spawned a huge range of merchandise, including dolls, toy stunt cycles, board games, t-shirts, record LPs, a pinball machine, posters, a Marvel comic book series and more.

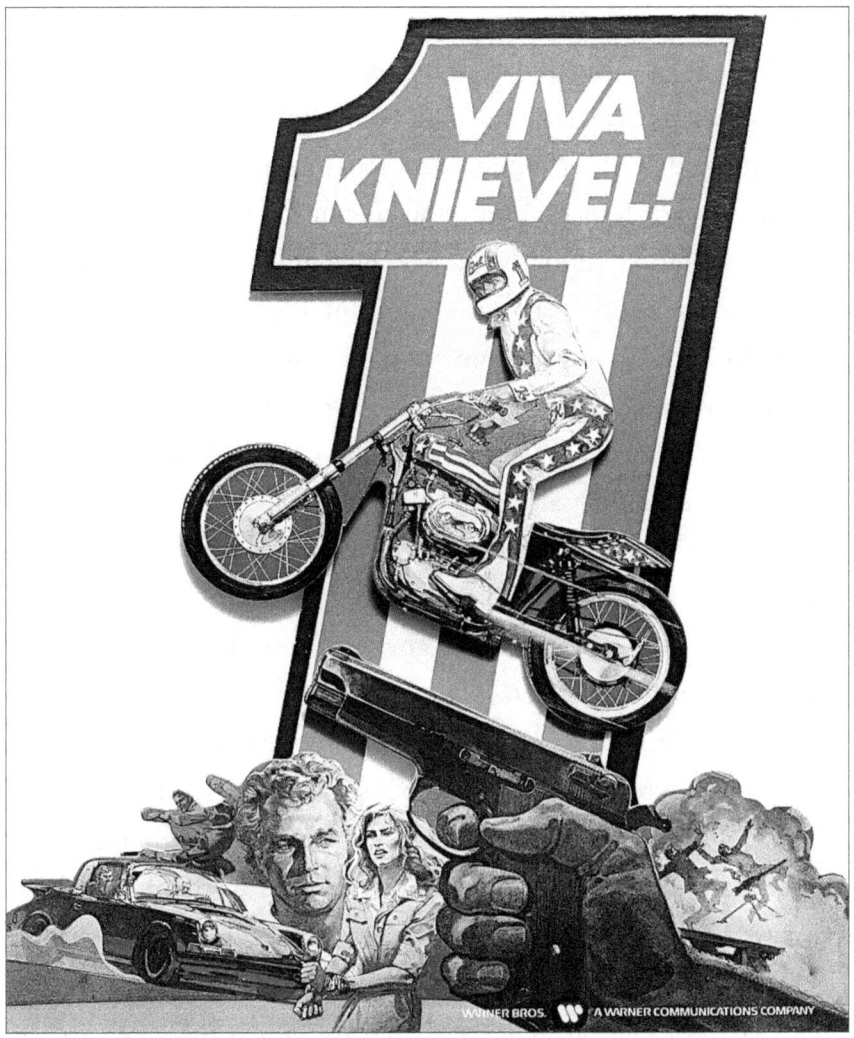

Promotional art for *Viva Knievel!*

Given Knievel's obvious love for—and mastery of—the art of self–promotion, it was only natural that his story would be put before the cameras sooner rather than later. The first Evel Knievel biopic was released in 1971 and was titled, surprisingly enough, *Evel Knievel*. Starring the perennially–tanned George Hamilton as Evel, and Sue Lyon from Stanley Kubrick's *Lolita* (1962) as his wife

Linda, and boasting a screenplay that was co-written by a young John Milius, *Evel Knievel* was a romanticized but entertaining look at the major events in Knievel's life up until that point, as well as his upbringing in Butte, Montana and relationship with his wife, and concluded with him hinting at an upcoming attempt at jumping across the Grand Canyon (a feat which would eventually materialize with his unsuccessful attempt at jumping the Snake River Canyon on his X-2 rocket Skycycle on September 8, 1974). A young Sam Elliott also played Knievel in a 1974 adventure/comedy TV movie, also titled *Evil Knievel*, which was a pilot for a planned television series that never went ahead.

A man with an enormous ego, George Hamilton claimed that Knievel was always bitter that he never got to portray himself in *Evel Knievel*, so six years later he got the chance to rectify that situation by starring as himself in *Viva Knievel!*, which was much more of a fictional story than the earlier film, and saw Evel really playing up to his self-created myth. The opening scene of the film sees Evel portraying himself as a mixture of Jesus Christ and Santa Claus, as he sneaks into a boys' orphanage in the dead of night, delivering presents to all the kids (Evel Knievel action figures, of course) and even performing a miracle cure on one of the poor crippled boys, who casts away his crutches and staggers across the room toward Evel, telling his hero that he will walk again just as Evel has walked again after his many famous accidents ("You're the reason I'm walking, Evel! You're the reason!").

His good deed out of the way, Evel and his aging, alcoholic mechanic Will Atkins (Gene Kelly) are busy preparing for his next big jump over an open-top cage filled with hungry lions and tigers, when Knievel is approached by feisty feminist photojournalist Kate Morgan (Lauren Hutton), who only seems interested in the event if there is a spectacular crash involved ("So they sent the chump out to shoot the champ?", Evel asks her disgustedly). As bad luck would have it, Evel does indeed crash his cycle upon completing his jump, an incident which he blames on Kate and her wishful thinking, then promptly announces his retirement before being shuffled off to hospital. While recuperating, Evel rejects all calls and offers to get back on his Harley-Davidson XR–750, until he gets coaxed out of his brief sabbatical by Jessie Hammond (Marjoe Gortner), a former protégé and now rival of Evel's, who convinces his one-time mentor to perform a big jump in Mexico for some mysterious financial backers that he is involved with. It all turns out to be a part of an elaborate plot to have Evel killed during the Mexico jump, then using an exact replica of his touring van to smuggle $30 million in cocaine back across the US border! As Knievel prepares for the massive jump (over a pit of fire), he is confronted by a clearly coked-out Jessie, who claims he is the rightful successor to Evel's fame and the superior jumper of the two. Determined to prove he is better, Jessie knocks Evel out in his trailer and dresses in his iconic red, white and blue jumpsuit, then takes his place at the jump ramp. Jesse successfully makes the jump, but is killed upon landing thanks to Evel's motorbike having been sabotaged by the bad guys. Knievel, of course, latches onto the plot, and after regaining consciousness and breaking Will free from a psych ward that he had been locked up in after stumbling upon the drug smuggling plot, defeats the criminals and wins the heart of Kate (though Knievel plays himself, no reference is ever made to his real-life wife or children).

Jessie (Marjoe Gortner, center) and Evel Knievel (himself, at right) have words in *Viva Knievel!*, while co–stars Leslie Nielsen and Gene Kelly look on.

Viva Knievel! was produced under the (uncredited) supervision of Irwin Allen, and Allen's wife Sheila also has a brief role in the film, playing Sister Charity who catches Evel sneaking into the orphanage and chastises him for waking all he boys up (Knievel quickly wins the full–figured Sister over with the promise of a box of her favorite chocolates). Marjoe Gortner as Jessie really nails the part of a rival stunt cycle rider, and he certainly looks resplendent in his mid–70s polyester attire of tight tan cotton pants and loud wide–collared red western shirt (though he comes in a distant second to Evel in the shirt collar stakes, with Knievel at one point walking around in a red silk shirt with collars so huge you would think a strong wind might scoop him up and carry him away at any moment). Gortner and Knievel have a pretty good chemistry together onscreen, most notably in the playful scene where Jessie visits Evel in the hospital after his accident, pushing him around the grounds in his wheelchair while trying to talk him out of his abrupt retirement. Former model Lauren Hutton helps bring a touch of class to the film, and given Evel's ego it's somewhat surprising that he allowed her character to be so demeaning of him and his stature at times ("I guess the jump is the exciting part", she deadpans after Knievel takes her for a few fast laps on the back of his bike), though Evel is quick to take a snide swipe at her feminist leanings when she says she prefers to be addressed as 'Ms' ("Oh, that makes you one of *them?*").

Supporting the quartet of leading actors are a number of familiar names and faces, including Leslie Nielsen as the unlikely drug lord who plans to use Knievel's Mexican jump as a ruse to transport his narcotics back across the border, Cameron Mitchell, comedian Red Buttons as a shonky jump promoter who puts ticket sales ahead of safety, and Dabney Coleman as the corrupt warden of the psychiatric unit that locks poor Will up in order to keep him separated from Evel.

A notorious consumer of alcohol, Evel uses *Viva Knievel!* to once again deliver his dramatically hilarious anti–drug speech, a variation of which he gave before his stunts over many years, without a hint of irony in regards to his own addictions:

"Before I make the jump, there's something I'd like to say to you, that's been bothering me for a long time.

I go to Indianapolis every year to see the Indy 500. I go there with friends to drive and race. Every year when they go there to qualify, they usually have to go as fast as they possibly can to get a front row position. They put nitro in their cars sometimes, instead of the fuel that is intended to be in the cars so that the cars will go faster…and they do, for five or ten laps. And then they blow all to hell.

And you people, you kids, if you put nitro in your bodies in the form of narcotics, so that you can do better, or so that maybe you think that you can do better, you will for about five or ten years, and then you'll blow all to hell."

For some of the more dangerous stunts in *Viva Knievel!*, professional stuntman Gary Charles Davis was brought in, although his participation in the film was kept tightly under wraps at the time of its release to help perpetuate the myth that it was Knievel himself performing all of his own onscreen stunt work.

Having its Hollywood premiere on 13 July 1977, *Viva Knievel!* was neither a critical or commercial success. The release of *Star Wars* (1977) just two months earlier ensured that just about every other film released during that American summer was going to struggle for attention. To make matters worse, in September of that year Knievel found himself embroiled in controversy when he assaulted sports promoter Shelly Saltman with a baseball bat, following the publication of *Evel Knievel on Tour*, an unauthorized book which Saltman had written based on information he had witnessed and tape recorded while he was working as a promoter for Knievel's Snake River Canyon jump. The resultant bad publicity, which saw Knievel lose a lot of his sponsorship and marketing deals, also stalled whatever little momentum which *Viva Knievel!* had, and it was pulled from the release schedule in several countries where it had not yet opened.

Viva Knievel! was the final film to be directed by Gordon Douglas, a New York native who started out as a child actor in several *Our Gang* shorts and whose long and varied filmography as a director included such works as *Zombies on Broadway* (1945), the classic atomic age monster movie *Them!* (1954), Elvis Presley's musical adventure *Follow that Dream* (1962), the Rat Pack mob caper *Robin and the 7 Hoods* (1964) and the Jerry Lewis comedy misfire *Way . . . Way Out* (1966). Douglas also helmed *In Like Flint*

(1967, a follow-up to the 1966 spy parody *In Like Flint*), *They Call Me Mister Tibbs!* (1970, the sequel to 1967's multi–Oscar–winning *In the Heat of the Night*) and the AIP blaxploitation film *Slaughter's Big Rip–Off* (1973, another sequel, this time to 1972's *Slaughter*).

SIDEWINDER 1
USA/September 21, 1977/96 minutes
Director: Earl Bellamy
Writers: Nancy Voyles Crawford & Thomas A. McMahon
Producer: Elmo Williams
Cast: Marjoe Gortner, Michael Parks, Susan Howard, Alex Cord & Charlotte Rae

Released by Avco Embassy, *Sidewinder 1* provided Marjoe Gortner with the opportunity to follow–up his work alongside Evel Knievel with yet another motorcycle–centric film, only this time taking top–billing in what was clearly a smaller production in terms of budget, but which managed to successfully capitalize on a thrill–seeking pastime which was then experiencing a particularly popular run in the United States.

Filmed in New Mexico (primarily Albuquerque and Taos) and set amongst the dirt–kicking world of motocross, *Sidewinder 1* has Marjoe playing Digger, a cocky and confident young motocross champion who is lured into a new partnership with businessman Packard Gentry (Alex Cord), who has financed the development of a new motorbike—the Sidewinder 1 of the title—which he believes will revolutionize the sport and dominate the competition. Joining Digger on Gentry's Sidewinder 1 team is J. W. Wyatt (Michael Parks), an older, more seasoned and cynical competitor riding the final laps of his professional career. Just when the team have ironed–out a few wrinkles and started pulling in some trophies, Gentry is killed when he takes the Sidewinder 1 for a rocky joyride without wearing a helmet and gets hit by another rider.

As Wyatt and Digger continue riding the Sidewinder 1 to success, tensions escalate between the riders and the rather prim and uppity Chris Gentry (Susan Howard), Packard's sister and now a majority shareholder in the motorbike. When Wyatt rejects Gentry's attempts to go along with the sale of the Sidewinder 1 to a Japanese businessman, she decides to take charge of her investment and accompany the two riders on their cross–country competition tour. While Digger enjoys his success with the local motocross groupies in each town, the ice between Gentry and Wyatt starts to predictably melt and the pair become intimately involved with each other, though it's not until Wyatt wraps up the championship (after Digger comes off his bike) that the pair's happily–ever–after future seems assured.

Released with a PG rating, *Sidewinder 1* runs very light on traditional exploitation drive–in elements like sex, nudity and violence, aiming to attract a more family–friendly crowd with its many motocross racing scenes, which are captured quite excitingly by cinematographer Dennis Dalzell. Motocross had been rising in popularity in the United States since the early–seventies (the first big motocross event being held at the Los Angeles Coliseum on July 8, 1972), making *Sidewinder 1* the first feature film to revolve around the sport (a fact happily pointed out in a lot of the promotional material issued for the movie). While the film is filled with lighthearted moments, a deliberate injection of humor is provided by the casting of Charlotte Rae, a familiar TV face and sit-com star, most notably in *Diff'rent Strokes* (1978–1986) and *The Facts of Life* (1979–1988), who plays Mrs. Holt, the pistol–mouthed but motherly manager of a competing motocross team who is not adverse to swinging her fists in the local bar in defense of her boys. Marjoe

Gortner, for his part, plays Digger like a college kid on summer vacation down in Florida, his most interesting scene being one where he belts out a rendition of "(Give Me That) Old–Time Religion." Though top–billed, Gortner pretty much plays support to Michael Parks and Susan Howard, a classy-looking actress best known for her recurring roles on the legal drama *Petrocelli* (1974–1976) and as Donna Culver Krebbs on *Dallas* (1978–1991).

Digger (Marjoe Gortner) and J. W. Wyatt (Michael Parks) discuss winning tactics in *Sidewinder 1*.

Sidewinder 1 was one of the last feature films from Earl Bellamy, a workhorse director with numerous episodic television shows under his belt, starting as far back as *Jungle Jim* in 1955. Bellamy would occasionally break out from television to helm the odd theatrical feature, perhaps most notably *Munster, Go Home!* (1966), the color film adaptation of *The Munsters* television series (1964–1966, of which Bellamy had also directed eight episodes). Bellamy also directed *Walking Tall, Part II* (1975) and *Sidecar Racers* (1975), an Australian production which, like *Sidewinder 1*, centered around the sport of motorbike racing. The same year as *Sidewinder 1*, he also helmed *Speedtrap* (1977), a somewhat obscure action adventure caper starring Joe Don Baker, Tyne Daly, Lana Wood and the amazing Timothy Carey (an actor I would have loved to have seen performing alongside Marjoe). Amongst Bellamy's TV movie work were the disaster double of *Flood!* (1976) and *Fire!* (1977), and *The Castaways on Gilligan's Island* (1979). The very dynamic original poster art for *Sidewinder 1* was painted by Robert Tanenbaum, an artist whose prolific filmography includes posters for *The Cycle Savages* (1969), *Battle for the Planet of the Apes* (1973), *Assault on Precinct 13* (1976), *Battlestar Galactica* (1978), *Meteor* (1979) and *Cujo* (1983).

WHEN YOU COMIN' BACK, RED RYDER
USA/February 9, 1979/118 minutes
Director: Milton Katselas
Writer: Mark Medoff
Producer: Marjoe Gortner
Cast: Marjoe Gortner, Candy Clark, Stephanie Faracy, Lee Grant, Hal Linden, Peter Firth, Pat Hingle, Audra Lindley & Bill McKinney

Based on an Obie Award–winning 1974 stage play by Mark Medoff (who also penned the screenplay for this cinematic adaptation), *When You Comin' Back, Red Ryder* is a hard film to categorize. Social commentary, psychological thriller, dark character study, seedy grindhouse exploitation film–all of these are applicable, yet none of them seem wholly suitable.

Set amongst the grim, depressing surrounds of a small New Mexico border town during the dying days of the 1960s, *When You Comin' Back, Red Ryder* casts Gortner as Teddy, a Vietnam vet with a high IQ and a silver tongue who takes out his violent frustrations, and unleashes all of his inner demons, on virtually anyone who crosses his path. Accompanied by his hippy chick girlfriend Cheryl (cult favorite Candy Clark), who is always being driven to her wits' end by Teddy's disturbing behavior, he rips off a quantity of cocaine from two Mexican drug dealers and hightails it back over the border, but not before deliberately toying with the customs officer, mockingly imitating his distinctive Southern drawl and answering his question of "Do you have anything to declare?" with "Two bottles of rum, and a considerable amount of cocaine." Teddy's little joke results in both Cheryl and himself being brought into the office and subjected to humiliating rectal exams, though the drugs hidden inside the generator of his VW van goes undetected.

Young hippie gal Cheryl (Candy Clark) gets in over her head when she hooks up with disturbed narcissist Teddy (Marjoe Gortner) in *When You Comin' Back, Red Ryder.*

Holing himself up inside a greasy roadside diner after his van breaks down not far over the border, Teddy decides to amuse himself by torturing—first psychologically, then physically—the small group of unfortunate inhabitants who just happen to be there when he arrives: Angel (the plump, naive waitress), Stephen 'Red' Ryder (the sour, angry night cook desperate to escape his stifling world), Lyle (the stroke-addled owner of the motel/gas station next to the diner) and Richard and Clarisse Ethridge (the repressed upper middle-class couple who are passing through on their way to a concerto that violinist Clarisse is performing in New Orleans).

At first little more than an annoying, insensitive nuisance, Teddy's behavior becomes increasingly mean spirited and violent, until he finally holds his unwitting audience in a vice-like grip of sheer terror and fearing for their lives. Despite his nastiness, Teddy has an uncanny ability to spot the weaknesses in people and recognize their true character. He admonishes Stephen for being a man out of time, his slicked-back hair, rolled-up shirt sleeves and cowboy boots, not to mention the "Born Dead" tattoo on his forearm, at striking odds with the peace and love movement being embraced by the majority of America's youth at the time. When Teddy discovers that Stephen was nicknamed "Red" when he was younger due to him having red hair as a child, he is both excited at the reference to Red Ryder, the old western cowboy icon, but disgusted that Stephen is not living up to the name with his cowardly ways.

By the end of the film, however, Teddy emerges almost as some kind of cathartic angel, though this interpretation is certainly open to debate, and there is an element of ambiguity to the ending. Prior to his arrival, all of the characters at the diner are portrayed as either lost, weak or tired souls, all unhappy and yearning for something else but lacking the courage to break out and reach for it. By

Teddy breaking down their will and forcing them to accept and face their own frailties and self-truths, they all ultimately emerge stronger for their ordeal (Angel and Red in particular), and ready to face the future with renewed confidence and honesty, or at least with an appreciation of what is actually important to them in their lives and relationships.

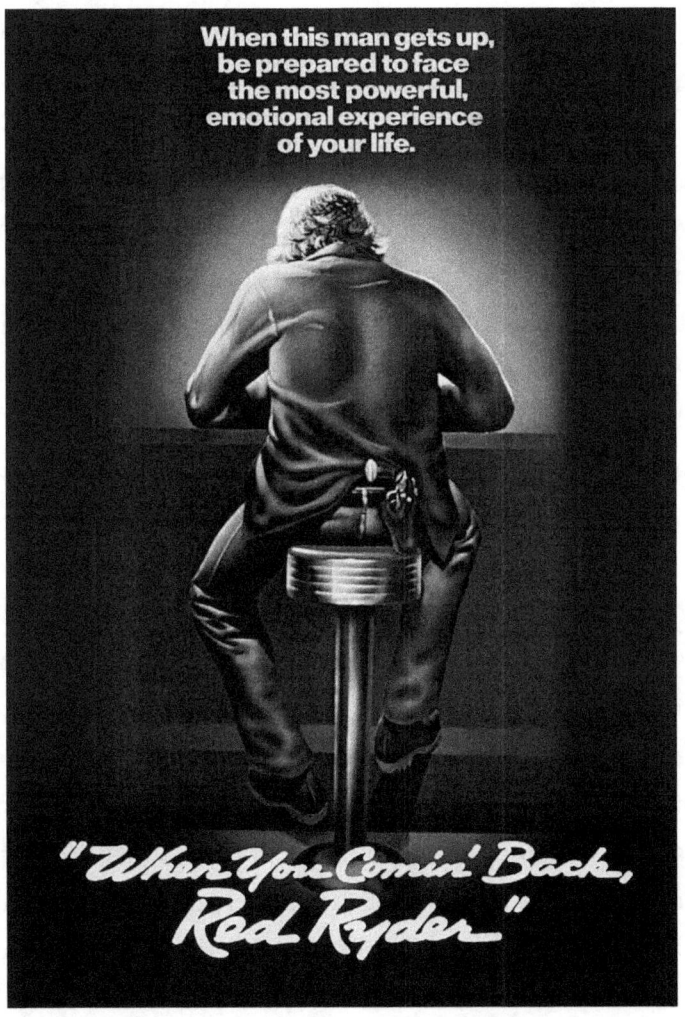

Stark and evocative poster art for *When You Comin' Back, Red Ryder*.

Along with dropping the question mark from the end of its title (effectively turning it into more of a statement than a question), one element of the film's narrative which differs significantly from the play is the climax. In Medoff's original play, Teddy has Red bind all the inhabitants of the diner before taking Richard's wallet and absconding, leaving the frightened and uncertain Cheryl behind. When the group are eventually discovered and freed by Tommy Clark, the diner's owner, who berates Red for not being more of a man in the situation, Red tells Clark where he can stick it, accepts Lyle's offer of a cash loan, then hitches a ride out of town with the Ethridges, presumably never to return. In the film, after Clark discovers the inhabitants of the diner and frees them from their bounds, Lyle indicates that Teddy is not likely to get far as he has rigged the replacement generator to burn out not long after it starts up. Clark berates Red as in the play, but in the film Red responds by telling Clark to stick the diner up his "rosy red rectum", then runs out of the diner and tears off after Teddy in Clark's pick-up truck, which is laden with a loaded shotgun. Red soon comes across Teddy's abandoned VW van on the outskirts of town, and finds Teddy himself sitting atop a nearby sand dune, seemingly waiting for his arrival. Strangely, Teddy removes his revolver from his coat pocket and hides it in a bag of groceries which he had packed and taken from the diner. Utilizing some slow–motion to heighten the suspense, as a young family picnic at the base of the sand dune, Red storms up the mound brandishing the shotgun, confronting Teddy and demanding he surrender to him. Remarkably, as if willing to sign his own death warrant in order to give Red the chance to prove himself, Teddy reaches into his empty jacket pocket as if going for his revolver. Clearly conflicted and pleading for Teddy to give up peacefully, Red eventually decides he cannot risk the outcome to chance and pulls the trigger on the shotgun, blowing a hole in the middle of Teddy's chest and sending his dead body rolling down the sand dune. We then see Red a week later, his hair growing out slightly and long-sleeved check shirt covering his tattoo, turning up to the diner in his new car, a black 1948 Mercury Eight. When Angel asks him how he could have afforded the new wheels, Red replies: "The price goes down if you're a hero." Red then announces he is leaving town for good and starts to drive off, leaving Angel in tears, before he suddenly stops and reverses back, telling Angel that he doesn't actually have a driver's license and offering her the chance to abandon her life at the diner and embark on an adventure with him, on the understanding that there will never be any kind of romantic relationship between the two of them. Angel considers for a moment, then runs into the diner to ditch her apron and have a last look around, before running back out to the car and sliding herself into the driver's seat and tearing off onto the main road and onto a new beginning, Red triumphantly pumping his fist in the air out of the passenger side window.

Despite its theatrical elements (the film's stage origins are certainly reflected here), *When You Comin' Back, Red Ryder* is full of memorable moments and passages of protracted tension and suspense, with director Milton Katselas making great use of the confined diner setting—where the majority of the film takes place—to create an effectively stifling and claustrophobic ambience. (As a piece of trivia, Milton Katselas was played by James Franco in *Sal*, the 2011 biopic of murdered actor Sal Mineo, which Franco also directed).

Without doubt, the strongest element of *When You Comin' Back, Red Ryder*, and the glue which holds the whole film together, is the galvanizing performance of Marjoe Gortner as Teddy. There can be little doubt that Marjoe utilized many of the tricks of body language, voice projection and eye contact that he employed as a preacher to bring Teddy to life with the depth that he does. He brings an incredible amount of menace to his character, along with an unpredictability that is terrifying, to both the audience and the characters around him. You never know what will set him off next, and his target will change at a moment's notice. Teddy derives a perverse joy in his belittling of others, and his psychological manipulation of those weaker than him.

Teddy (Marjoe Gortner) menaces Clarisse Ethridge (Lee Grant) as husband Richard (Hal Linden) looks on helplessly in *When You Comin' Back, Red Ryder*.

A lot of the thematic power of *When You Comin' Back, Red Ryder* comes from the way it deconstructs the counterculture ideals of late–sixties America. Teddy and Cheryl look every bit the quintessential young hippy couple, but only Cheryl acts the part. When Richard Ethridge, reacting to Teddy's verbal and physical abuse, asks him "Whatever happened to all that peace and love garbage?', Teddy replies:

"Well, that was another group, sir. That was those other fellas. No, we ain't in favor of love and peace."

While it is Marjoe who clearly dominates the film, *When You Comin' Back, Red Ryder* also boasts a very fine supporting cast, including the previously noted Candy Clark (1976's *The Man Who Fell to Earth* and the 1988 remake of *The Blob*), Hal Linden from the long–running sit–com *Barney Miller* (1975–1982) as Richard Ethridge, and a magnificent Lee Grant as his wife Clarisse. Grant would be familiar to fans of 1970s studio genre films through her work in *Airport '77* (1977), *The Swarm* (1978) and *Damien: Omen II* (1978). There's also Pat Hingle (a veteran of several Clint Eastwood films and Commissioner Gordon in the 1990s *Batman* movies) as Lyle and Bill McKinney as diner owner Tommy Clark. So good in the carnival–set exploitation classic *She-Freak* (1967), McKinney is perhaps best known as the creepy hillbilly who rode poor Ned Beatty into the mud and made him "Squeal like a pig" in John Boorman's *Deliverance* (1972). Relative unknowns Stephanie Faracy and Peter Firth hold their own amongst this strong ensemble, and as Angel and Red Ryder respectively have some strong scenes and a great chemistry together. Audra Lindley also has some nice moments as Ceil Ryder, Red's lonely and used mother, while acclaimed musician and songwriter Leon Russell provides the memorable voice of the radio preacher heard as background white noise. Mark Medoff himself also appears in the film, appearing as a faith healer during a church ceremony.

Filmed in El Paso, cinematographer Jules Brenner really catches the grimy roadside diner ambience, as well as the heat and barren dustiness of the external locations, and a genuine feel of Small

Town, USA. Brenner also photographed the TV mini-series *Helter Skelter* (1976), which documented the infamous Charles Manson killings, and Tobe Hooper's TV adaptation of Stephen King's *Salem's Lot* (1979), as well as Dan O'Bannon's classic horror/comedy *The Return of the Living Dead* (1984). The film also boasts a terrific soundtrack featuring cuts by The Doors ("People Are Strange"), Tammy Wynette ("Kiss Away"), B.B. King ("The Thrill is Gone"), Boots Randolph ("Tequila") and others, while the great Jack Nitzsche provides the atmospheric instrumental music. Soundtrack licensing issues are supposedly one of the major reasons why *When You Comin' Back, Red Ryder* has been so hard to find in the years following its release. The film did appear on home video in the 1980s in some countries (including a rare release in Australia on the Roadshow label), and a DVD release also appeared in Australia in 2014 on the Umbrella Entertainment label, which was great to see even though it was a bare bones release utilizing a fairly grainy print that looked to have been struck from an old VHS master. In Australia, the film received a brief theatrical release under the rather generic title of *Getting Even*, while in Argentina it was released on home video in 1990 as *Perversion*.

When You Comin' Back, Red Ryder also represented Marjoe's first foray into feature film production, with Gortner securing the $1.8 million production costs from shopping mall tycoon Melvin Simon. Simon had entered film production the year before, as an uncredited producer on William Girdler's supernatural horror *The Manitou* (1978), and although he later claimed that he made a big mistake by getting into the film business, he did end up producing a number of box-office successes, including *Love at First Bite* (1979), *When a Stranger Calls* (1979) and the teen sex comedy hit *Porky's* (1981) and its two sequels.

Actor/producer Marjoe Gortner and director Milton Katselas conferring behind the scenes on *When You Comin' Back, Red Ryder.*

You'd have to wonder whether Marjoe looks back upon *When You Comin' Back, Red Ryder* as something of a bittersweet experience. While the film has attained a devoted—if still rather small—band of passionate cult followers in the ensuing years, it did not do well financially upon its release and proved to be Marjoe's first and last attempt at feature film production. The period also marked an important time in Marjoe's personal life, having gotten involved in an intense romantic relationship with co-star Candy Clark in 1977, an affair which quickly led to the pair skipping across the border from Texas to Mexico for a quickie $60 wedding at a registry office in the town of Zaragoza. Unfortunately, the marriage was a very short-lived one, with the couple separating in December of 1979. An article on the newly-married couple by Lois Armstrong which appeared in the June 26, 1978 issue of *People* magazine hinted that the coupling may not have been fully thought out.

"We loitered for an hour with newspapers and dust blowing all around us, trying to make up our minds to go in," (Candy) Clark says. "People drove by honking because they could see what was happening. The sun started to go down, couldn't decide yes or no anymore. I was in a maybe state."

The article goes on to end on a rather prophetic note:

'A friend who didn't yet know Clark and Gortner were married predicted their romance wouldn't outlive the Ryder shooting. Gortner himself jokes, "This marriage might last six or eight months." She ripostes, "I'm going to pick his brain while it lasts."'

A remarkable piece of work, *When You Comin Back, Red Ryder* is truly one of the unsung masterpieces of 1970s American cinema, a film whose appraisal is long overdue and one of the seminal moments in the Marjoe Gortner filmography. Sadly, Mark Medoff, who also penned the screenplay for the early Chuck Norris action flick *Good Guys Wear Black* (1978) as well as the Tony-winning *Children of a Lesser God* for the stage in 1980, passed away on 23 April, 2019. Medoff also wrote a sequel to *When You Comin' Back, Red Ryder* titled *The Heart Outright*. Premiering on stage in 1986, *The Heart Outright* catches up with Stephen "Red" Ryder as a Vietnam Vet in his late-twenties who now manages a porno cinema in Texas before returning to his home town for his mother's funeral and having to confront Angel and the demons left from his heroic actions of the past. A low-budget film adaptation of *The Heart Outright* was directed in 2016 by Medoff's son-in-law Ross Kagan Marks and featured his daughter Jessica Medoff in the role of Angel.

STARCRASH
Italy–USA/March 9, 1979/94 minutes
Director: Luigi Cozzi (as Lewis Coates)
Writers: Nat Wachsberger & Luigi Cozzi (as Lewis Coates)
Producers: Nat Wachsberger & Patrick Wachsberger
Cast: Marjoe Gortner, Caroline Munro, Judd Hamilton, Robert Tessier, Christopher Plummer, David Hasselhoff & Joe Spinell

The enormous (and somewhat unexpected) box-office success that greeted George Lucas' space opera *Star Wars* when it was first released in the US in May of 1977, created a social and pop culture phenomenon which triggered a resurgence of interest in all things science-fiction and sent independent and exploitation producers scrambling to cash-in with their own space adventure quickies. Japan produced a *Message from Space* (1978), Disney took us through *The Black Hole* (1979), Glen A. Larsen brought space into the small screen with television's *Battlestar Galactica* and Roger Corman got to work on creating a *Battle Beyond the Stars* (1980).

In Italy, a country whose movie studios were known to capitalize on trends which they saw coming across from the US, the task of creating a spaghetti *Star Wars* fell upon the shoulders of Luigi Cozzi, a young (31 at the time) horror and sci-fi buff who had written reports on Italian genre films for *Famous Monsters of Filmland* magazine, and whose first film credit of note was writing the original story from which Dario Argento's giallo thriller *Four Flies on Grey Velvet* (1971) was adapted. Cozzi's genuine love of fantasy cinema made him a natural choice to deliver an Italian space adventure film, but because he had not yet actually seen *Star Wars* (it had not yet been released in that country) he had to turn to the films that had inspired him during his childhood and teenage years, as well as the paperback novelization of *Star Wars,* which was published six months prior to the film's release, to provide the inspiration for his screenplay (which he wrote in collaboration with co–producer Nat Wachsberger).

The resultant film, Starcrash (aka The Adventures of Stella Star) was a colorful amalgamation of Barbarella (1968) and classic Ray Harryhausen, with a sexy, scantily–clad leading character romping her way through a story and sets that mixed saucy Euro comic book fantasy with Saturday morning live–action kiddie television. The film stars cult British actress Caroline Munro as Stella Star, a leggy and provocatively–dressed intergalactic smuggler who, along with her alien companion Akton (Marjoe Gortner) is recruited by the Emperor of the Galaxy (Christopher Plummer) to rescue his son Prince Simon (David Hasselhoff) and destroy a deadly secret weapon which has been developed by the evil Count Zarth Arn (Joe Spinell). Along the way, Stella and Akton encounter female Amazonian warriors, a tribe of barbarians, robot golems and a variety of other intergalactic menaces. And of course, Stella ends up falling in love with Prince Simon.

Original American one-sheet poster for *Starcrash*.

Filming of Starcrash took place at the famous Cinecittà Studios in Rome as well as Hollywood and locations in Tunisia and Morocco. As the alien Akton, Marjoe brings an interesting performance to the film . . . unemotional, scientific and rational, very much in the mold of Mr. Spock (Leonard Nimoy) in the *Star Trek* television series and motion pictures. Originally, Luigi Cozzi had envisioned Akton as having a less human visage, and intended to use prosthetic make–up to enhance his features. But when Marjoe arrived on the set in Rome, he refused to have any part of his face covered, ultimately playing the character more like a detached and unemotional human rather than an obvious alien, which creates an interesting dynamic between Akton and Stella Star, one that is totally devoid of any sexual chemistry or tension (it's likely a lot of viewers may have questioned Akton's sexuality, since he never shows any interest in the alluring and provocatively dressed Stella). The screenplay gives Akton a number of special powers which seems to vary without explanation depending on what he needs according to any given situation, and his laser sword weapon is clearly inspired by the famous *Star Wars* lightsabers. Slim and dressed throughout in a shiny red and black jumpsuit, some of the original posters for *Starcrash* depicted Marjoe's character as very muscular, barrel–chested and dressed in little more than a pair of boots and tight wrestling shorts!

Featuring a soundtrack by veteran James Bond composer John Barry, *Starcrash* was a decent crowd pleaser with cinema audiences around the world (primarily young boys and men wanting to get an eyeful of Caroline Munro), but despite talk a sequel never eventuated. The film, though, does have a strong and loyal cult following. It is one of the most entertaining of the original wave of *Star Wars* cash–ins, is a favorite of stoners thanks to its gaudy color pal–

ate, and has a terrific cast that features a fascinating assortment of one-time Hollywood heavyweights (Christopher Plummer), future stars (a pre-*Baywatch* David Hasselhoff) and notorious character actors (Joe Spinell, who would go on to co-write and star—alongside Caroline Munro—in William Lustig's notoriously sleazy and violent *Maniac* in 1980). Munro herself was known at the time for her appearances in British horror and fantasy films such as *The Abominable Dr. Phibes* (1971), *Dracula A.D. 1972* (1972), *The Golden Voyage of Sinbad* (1973), *Captain Kronos—Vampire Hunter* (1974), *At the Earth's Core* (1976) and the James Bond adventure *The Spy Who Loved Me* (1977). In *Starcrash*, Munro's husband at the time, Judd Hamilton, played Elle, a robot policeman with human emotions.

Luigi Cozzi on Marjoe Gortner

After helming *Starcrash*, Luigi Cozzi would co-write and direct the notorious *Alien* (1979)-inspired *Contamination* (aka *Alien Contamination*, 1980), as well as *Hercules* (1983) and its sequel *The Adventures of Hercules* (1985), the later two starring Lou Ferrigno as the titular hero. Most of his films were credited to his Lewis Coates pseudonym for their releases outside of Italy. Cozzi continues to write and direct and develop projects in his home country, as well as running his Profondo Rosso film memorabilia store in Rome.

How did Marjoe come to be cast in Starcrash? Was he someone who was on your radar that you had in mind for the film, or was he recommended to you by someone?
The cast of *Starcrash* was mainly assembled through ICM Agency in Los Angeles. But Marjoe was hired for a different reason: in the beginning *Starcrash* was due to be released through AIP (American International Pictures) and, having recently starred in the AIP box

office hit *The Food of the Gods*, Marjoe was actually put in my cast by Sam Arkoff, also considering the fact that in the meantime Marjoe had established a very good friendship with Arkoff's son, Lou.

What was Marjoe like to work with, and how did he behave on set?
Marjoe was very collaborative and helpful during the shooting of *Starcrash*. He had fun working on it and I had a very good relationship with him. There were never problems or troubles of any sort, and I think he did a very good acting job.

Luigi Cozzi directs Marjoe Gortner and Caroline Munro on the set of *Starcrash*.

Were you aware of his background as a child preacher and evangelist when you hired him, or did you know him purely from his acting roles that he had begun to undertake in the 1970s?
I absolutely had no idea that Marjoe had a past as child preacher.

For me he was just an actor and the star of *The Food of the Gods*. I was informed about his past as a child evangelist only midway through the shooting of the movie, when Joe Spinell told me something about it.

Did Marjoe have much input into the development of his character once he came on board Starcrash? I believe his character was supposed to originally wear a mask or make–up, but Marjoe refused to cover his face?

The character of Akton, which Marjoe had been hired to play, was to be a totally alien creature, humanoid in shape but with a completely non–human face. This was because in my writing I wanted Stella Star to really stand out as a human being above her two very "different" comrades, an alien (Akton) and a robot. But when I met Marjoe in the hotel immediately after his arrival in Rome, he told me he simply refused to wear any kind of makeup on his face. Obviously, this changed completely the situation which was written in the script. I thought a night over it and then decided not to clash against AIP and Sam Arkoff (who absolutely had wanted Marjoe in the cast) and so I decided to agree with Marjoe's will. I accepted the fact that he was not going to wear any heavy alien makeup on his face but as a substitution to this I decided to give Akton very special ESP and superhuman mind powers. I explained this new proposal of mine to Marjoe and he liked it, so I proceeded to modify the screenplay accordingly, and the final result really satisfied me (and Marjoe too).

Did you stay in touch with Marjoe after work on Starcrash wrapped?

I shot in a Cinecittà studio the last scene with Marjoe (the one which is at the very beginning of the movie) just before wrapping principal photography, a week before Christmas 1977. Marjoe was due to leave Rome the very next day, so after the shooting we embraced and exchanged the best Christmas wishes, and then he left. Since then I've not heard from him anymore. But I still remember him as a kind, nice person and a good, very professional player who gave a strong contribution to turn my *Starcrash* into the little cult movie it has become worldwide.

MAUSOLEUM
USA/May 13, 1983/96 Minutes
Director: Michael Dugan
Writers: Robert Barich & Robert Madero
Producers: Robert Barich & Robert Madero
Cast: Marjoe Gortner, Bobbie Bresee, Norman Burton, Maurice Sherbanee, LaWanda Page & Julie Christy Murray

The early–eighties were a great time to be a young horror movie fan. The home video revolution put more viewing choices before us than ever before, providing the chance to finally see films only previously read about (or only seen on television in cut–down prints). Newer theatrical hits like *The Evil Dead* (1981) and the *Friday the 13th* series also benefited greatly from the home video format, and helped spawn a rash of imitators who were all looking for a slice of the splatter pie. Gore was big, special effects artists like Tom Savini and Dick Smith were the new horror cult figures, and *Fangoria* was there to capture and help promote it all within the pages of their semi–glossy newsstand magazine.

Written and produced by two Roberts, Barich and Madero (Barich also served as cinematographer), *Mausoleum* is pretty reflective of the low–budget, independent American horror scene of the time, at least in terms of tone and production values. The film cobbles together a story inspired by the demonic possession craze of a decade earlier, and adds some *Evil Dead*–like comic book gore and demonic transformations, then ticks off the remaining exploitation boxes with some smatterings of sex and nudity. The film opens in a cemetery, where ten–year–old Susan Nomed (Julie Christy Murray) is standing over the fresh grave of her mother under the watchful eye of Aunt Cora (Laura Hippe). When Susan suddenly runs off from her aunt, a strange fog descends and compels her to enter the mausoleum of the Nomed family, where a demonic cloaked figure waves its hand and causes Susan's eyes to glow a radioactive green (the mysterious figure also causes the head of a nosey cemetery caretaker to explode).

Lurid French poster art for *Mausoleum*.

Cut to twenty years later, and Susan Nomed has grown into Susan Farrell (Bobbie Bresee), a beautiful blonde woman in her early–thirties married to successful executive Oliver Farrell (Marjoe Gortner) and living the American Dream in a nice big house. But as soon as we cut to psychiatrist Dr. Simon Andrews (Norman Burton) telling Aunt Cora that her concerns for Susan's safety and sanity are unfounded, we know bad things are about to start happening, as Cora starts filling us all in on 300–year–old demonic curse that supposedly haunts the Nomed family (of course, in a nod to the famous Count Alucard, you only have to say the Nomed's family name backwards to realize they are doomed). Things start going haywire for Susan later that evening, when Oliver takes her out to blow off a bit of steam on the disco dancefloor. Disgusted after being hit on by a drunk Grizzly Adams lookalike, Susan later kills the unwanted suitor by making his car catch fire with her glowing eyes.

Next on Susan's hit list is Ben (Maurice Sherbanee), the sleazy gardener who is always leering at Susan and peering in on what she and Oliver are up to. With her husband at work, Susan gives Ben a little flash of flesh from the upstairs patio, before leading him into the garage for sex, after which her inner demon once again emerges and poor Ben is ripped apart with a metal gardening rake. Susan quickly moves on to Aunt Cora, whom she levitates through the house before using her powers to rip her chest open while she is still suspended in mid-air (thanks to the matting, in most DVD and VHS prints of the film, the mechanism used to suspend and move Laura Hippe though the air is clearly visible at the top of the frame, though it has been rectified in the 2019 Blu–ray release from Vinegar Syndrome). It's here that we finally get our first good look at Susan's demonic alter-ego, thanks to a pretty decent makeup effects job by the late John Carl Buechler, who was still in the early days of his career here but would soon become something of a *Fangoria* favorite thanks to his work on movies like *Ghoulies* (1984), *From Beyond* (1986), *Friday the 13th Part VII: The New Blood* (1988) and *A Nightmare on Elm Street 4: The Dream Master* (1988).

While he seems to be enjoying a wilder sex life than usual, Oliver becomes increasingly concerned about his wife's erratic and disturbing behavior, despite the reassurances of Dr. Andrews. Even the maid knows things aren't as they seem. "There's some strange shit going on in this house", she mutters under her breath before hightailing it out the door with her bags packed. Dr. Andrews is finally convinced that something is very wrong with Susan when her demonic alter–ego emerges while she is under hypnosis in his office, forcing him to seek help from a more suitably trained colleague ("I'm not in the habit of seeing my clients light–up", he explains). Susan meanwhile continues on her merry evil way, killing a delivery boy who thinks he is in for some mature lovin', and then sends an art gallery owner to his splattery demise in a shopping mall before stealing a rather macabre piece of original art.

"What the hell is this?!", Oliver demands when he lays eyes on the demonic, sub-Frank Frazetta painting which Susan has brought home to liven up the décor. The dish–smashing argument which ensues soon turns into a romantic interlude after Oliver catches sight of Susan soaking in a bubble bath. Hugging her slippery and soapy naked body against him, Oliver and Susan begin to kiss passionately until—in one of the film's real highlights—Susan's inner demon emerges and her breasts, now transformed into demon faces with sharp teeth and hungry mouths, eat their way through Oliver's chest cavity and devour his heart. In shock and with his ribs poking out from the gaping wound in his chest, Oliver falls back dead into the bath, a look of complete astonishment frozen on his face.

With just about everyone around her now either dead or scared right off, it falls to Dr. Andrews to save Susan from the Nomed curse, which he does by retrieving a crown of thorns from the mausoleum and placing it upon her head, driving the demonic spirit out of Susan as promised within the pages of a secret family diary that he had been made privy to. Though Susan's demonic alter ego teleports itself back to the family mausoleum where it apparently dies, the final shot of the film reveals that the hooded new caretaker of the crypt is none other than Ben the sleazy gardener whom had earlier been horribly murdered by Susan's demonic self during their tryst in the garage! Exactly what this revelation means is up to the audience to interpret, but it makes about as much sense as anything else in the movie, and helps make it reminiscent of the classic twist endings as often seen in the notorious EC horror comics of the early-fifties. In fact, with its lurid green and purple lighting and fog-bound sets (even indoors), the whole film often evokes the feel of a pulpy four-color horror comic. The interior of the mausoleum set was designed by Robert A. Burns, who had so effectively turned a remote farmhouse into a stifling house of horrors with his work on Tobe Hooper's *The Texas Chainsaw Massacre* (1974).

In one of his last real leading feature film roles, Marjoe Gortner gets to play somewhat against type in *Mausoleum*, his Oliver being a decent man with a good job who is trying his best to have a happy marriage to Susan. Unfortunately, Marjoe tries to play the nice guy a little too earnestly, coming off a bit weak and wishy washy as a result. He does succeed in at least making you feel a little sorry for the poor guy, as you know he is trying his best but is bound to not make it through to the end of the movie alive. And once again we have the interesting situation where the one-time preacher of God's word is now finding his on-screen celluloid character confronting a satanic evil.

Oliver Farrell (Marjoe Gortner) offers comfort to his possessed wife Susan (Bobbie Bresee) in *Mausoleum*.

Though nothing like a huge hit, *Mausoleum* proved to be quite popular with younger horror fans at the time, especially as a home video rental. Much of the film's original promotion centered on its female star, Bobbie Bresee, a former Playboy Bunny who became something of a short-lived "scream queen" in the mid–eighties thanks to her role in *Mausoleum* and other cult horror films like *Ghoulies* (1984), *Surf Nazies Must Die* (1987) and *Evil Spawn* (1987). Already in her mid–thirties when she started her career in horror films, after making her early appearances on a number of episodic TV shows between 1978–1982, Bresee retired from acting in 1995. A close friend of *Famous Monsters of Filmland* editor Forrest J. Ackerman, Bresee posed with Ackerman (wearing a Frankenstein's monster mask) for the cover of the 1986 one-shot publication *Forrest J. Ackerman: Famous Monster of Filmland* (a cover which paid homage to the cover of the first issue of *Famous Monsters* from 1958). In 1979, while trying to launch her movie career, she made headlines at the Cannes Film Festival by attending an event clearly braless behind a tiny, sheer black top.

JUNGLE WARRIORS

West German–Mexico/May 11, 1984 (West Germany)/155 minutes
Director: Ernst R. von Theumer
Writers: Robert Collector & Ernst R. von Theumer
Producer: Ernst R. von Theumer
Cast: Nina van Pallandt, Paul L. Smith, John Vernon, Alex Cord, Sybil Danning, Marjoe Gortner & Woody Strode
AKA: Jungle Fever, The Czar of Brazil, Your Path Leads Through Hell

While foreign jungles have always provided a suitable backdrop for movie thrills (thanks in no small part to a steady stream of Tarzan movies produced during the 1930s–1960s), the setting became a lot more exotic and foreboding in the seventies and eighties. The early-seventies saw Roger Corman take advantage of cheap labor and tax breaks to produce a string of Women in Prison films in the steamy Filipino jungle, while Italian cannibal movies set deep in the South American Amazon provided grindhouse audiences with some gory thrills later in the decade. The mid-eighties also saw a rise in American productions taking an exploitative view of the still-stinging Vietnam jungle war, spearheaded by the success of *Missing in Action* (1984) and *Rambo: First Blood Part II* (1985).

Shot in Mexico and West Germany, but set in South America, *Jungle Warriors* is one of the lesser-known films in the eighties jungle genre, and a movie that sadly wastes a nice eclectic cast on a mostly unexciting tale of coke-sniffing American model agency exec Larry Schecter (Marjoe Gortner), who arrives in South America with a string of his stunning model clients to oversee a photo shoot taking place in the tropical Peruvian forest. Unfortunately, their small seaplane is shot down by notorious drug lord Cesar Santiago (Paul L. Smith) when it flies over his cocaine plantation. Though all onboard survive the emergency landing, they are soon fighting hard to stay one step ahead of Santiago's vicious guerilla army while also dealing with giant anacondas and other deadly dangers of the jungle. When Schecter is killed by a spiked jungle trap and all of the five models, along with their guardian Joanna (Nina Van Pallandt) and a blonde that Schecter had picked up the night before, are captured by Santiago's grotty men, it's up to them to save themselves before they outlive their usefulness and are executed. A subplot involves an American mob boss named Vito Mastranga (John Vernon) and his henchman nephew (Alex Cord) arranging a deal with Santiago to swap gold for cocaine, and of course one of the captured women turns out to be an undercover drug enforcement agent working on a case to bust the cartel apart.

Santiago may have a big operation going but a lot of his hired muscle are pretty weak and security lax, as the captured women are able to escape their cell, arm themselves and penetrate Santiago's fortress with considerable ease. Mastering the use of their weaponry within seconds, our heroines start spraying Santiago's compound with bullets in an orgy of gunfire that escalates with the arrival of the drug enforcement agents, and culminates with Santiago being blown out of the sky with a rocket launcher while trying to flee the carnage in his helicopter.

Unfortunately, *Jungle Warriors* treads its ground too timidly for this genre, so it succeeds neither as an exploitation grindhouse flick nor an entertaining low-budget actioner. There is not a whole lot of nudity or blood, though there is an extended and unpleasant prison gang rape sequence as well as one inventive moment of violence when the ape-like Santiago kills the John Vernon character by putting him on a detached car door like a turkey on a dinner plate and then lifting him up into the deadly whirring blades of a helicopter. The rape sequence was later deleted, and the helicopter death and Schecter's killing trimmed of all blood, for the movie's subsequent re-releases and television broadcasts, and this edited print has also found its way onto several home video releases of the film (the shorter versions of the film run approximately 82 minutes as opposed to the uncut 93 minute print).

Marjoe Gortner was only brought into *Jungle Warriors* at the last minute, in fact while the production was already underway. The supporting role of Larry Schecter was originally given to notorious Hollywood hellraiser Dennis Hopper, who upon arriving on location in Cuernavaca, Mexico, immediately got stone drunk on complementary tequila before tearing off all of his clothes and running off naked into the jungle, screaming that World War III had broken out. Hopper, who blamed his psychotic breakdown on the hotel tequila, which he claimed had been laced with LSD, was sent back to the United States to begin a nightmarish detox while Marjoe Gortner was quickly flown in to take his place in front of the cameras. Schecter is certainly the kind of character that you could see Hopper taking in a manic direction, but Marjoe plays him rather straightforward and reserved, perhaps as a result of coming into the project late and not having much time to work on developing his own take on the character. Nevertheless, Gortner still fits in well with the rest of the cast, and his physique makes him look more suitably fit for the jungle than what Hopper might have been at that point. Of course, Hopper had played a manic photojournalist in Francis Ford Coppola's Vietnam War classic *Apocalypse Now* (1979), so it's possible to speculate that he may have referenced that character had he gone on to play Larry Schecter.

Exciting poster art for *Jungle Warriors*, which the film itself sadly fails to match.

Taking the acting honors in *Jungle Warrior* are Paul L. Smith as Cesar Santiago and buxom glamazon Sybil Danning as his sister and brutal second-in-command, Angel. Certainly an odd couple, there is a blatant incestuous edge to the relationship between these siblings, with Cesar at one point treating his naked sister to a butt massage! Cesar does quickly clarify at one point late in the movie that Angel is in fact only his half-sister, just to ensure that things don't come off as too icky for the censors. The choice of Paul L. Smith as Cesar is inspired, with the burly Bud Spencer look-a-like delivering the same shifty-eyed expressions that made his red-herring character in the Spanish/Italian gore classic *Pieces* (1982) so memorable. Although he had a face and physique that was made for them, Smith's career wasn't limited to the low-budget exploitation genres, with the Massachusetts-born actor also appearing in Alan Parker's harrowing *Midnight Express* (1978), as well as playing Bluto in Robert Altman's *Popeye* (1980) opposite Robin Williams and Shelly Duvall. He also had a role in David Lynch's lavish but highly divisive *Dune* (1984). Austrian-born director Ernst Ritter von Theumer had previously used both Danning and John Vernon in a movie which he had executive produced, the trashy babes-behind-bars classic *Chained Heat* (1983), which was much more successful at blending its exploitation elements than *Jungle Warriors*.

One of the stranger highlights of *Jungle Warriors* is its opening theme song, performed by young Italian female singer Marina Arcangeli, whose style seemed to be a mix of new wave and rock delivered with a dramatic and throaty vocal style. Not much is known about Arcangeli, but she was popular enough to have a number of records released in Italy and Germany during the 1980s, and appeared on several television shows in those countries. Her theme song for *Jungle Warriors* is simply called "Song" in the end credits but is likely called "Heat", considering the amount of time she sings that word throughout. While it may seem like a wholly inappropriate tune to introduce a tacky jungle exploitation flick, on its own it's a strangely compelling track which uses as its base the American female rock of that period (such as Pat Benatar and Joan Jett) and puts a more avant–garde Euro–pop layer over the top of it, with Arcangeli's husky, tortured vocals sounding as if she recorded the song on her suicide death bed (which I say as a compliment as her voice absolutely makes the song quite unique). The song is repeated during the film's closing shots and over the end titles.

HELLHOLE
USA/April 26, 1985/90 minutes
Director: Pierre De Moro
Writer: Aaron Butler
Producers: Lou Arkoff & Billy Fine
Cast: Ray Sharkey, Judy Landers, Marjoe Gortner, Marneen Fields, Mary Woronov, Richard Cox, Edy Williams, Terry Moore, Dyanne Thorne & Robert Z'Dar

Along with the Blaxploitation films, epitomized by titles like *Shaft* (1971), *Super Fly* (1972) and *Black Caesar* (1973), one of the most popular staples of early 1970's American drive–ins and grindhouse cinemas were the Women in Prison movies (or WIP, as they endearingly came to be referred to by fans). Bearing names like *The Big Doll House* (1971), *Sweet Sugar* (1972) and Jonathan Demme's *Caged Heat* (1974), the WIP genre fed its audience a faithful diet of sex, violence, all–girl shower sequences and semi–naked catfights.

In the early 1980s, the WIP film made something of a temporary comeback, thanks primarily to the emerging home video market and its audience hungry for cheap thrills, along with the success of Paul

Nicholas' cult hit *Chained Heat*, starring Linda Blair, Sybil Danning and John Vernon. The success of *Chained Heat* led to a new spate of WIP films hitting the market over the ensuing few years, including *Red Heat* (1985, once again starring Linda Blair), and Tom DeSimone's much more comic book–esque *Reform School Girls* (1986).

Released in March of 1985, *Hellhole* may have been a late arrival in the 80s WIP cycle, but it certainly made up for its lateness by being a rather strange and uniquely outrageous addition to the genre. The film itself is set not behind the cold metal bars of a female prison or reformatory school, but within the walls of the Ashland Sanitarium for Women, where doe–eyed blonde Barbie doll Susan (Judy Landers) has been committed after witnessing her mother's murder and going completely blank on the incident. Unfortunately, the person responsible for the killing, a lowlife sleazeball named Silk (Ray Sharkey) did not retrieve what he was sent there to obtain (a bunch of bank statements that Susan's mother stole that are incriminating towards her shady boss), and he infiltrates the sanitarium as an orderly in the hopes of being able to jog Susan's memory on the whereabouts of the damning papers. Once behind the doors of the Ashland Sanitarium, we are exposed to all the seedy goings on within its seemingly respectable walls, including the usual lesbian sex, rampant drug use and naked shower scenes, as well as its most feared secret: the Hellhole, a separate fenced–off area of the sanitarium where patients who misbehave are sent to and never come back from. Once condemned to the Hellhole, the poor girls are subjected to the bizarre experimentations of Dr. Fletcher (Mary Woronov) and Dr. Miles Dane (Marjoe Gortner), who are fooling around with chemical lobotomies.

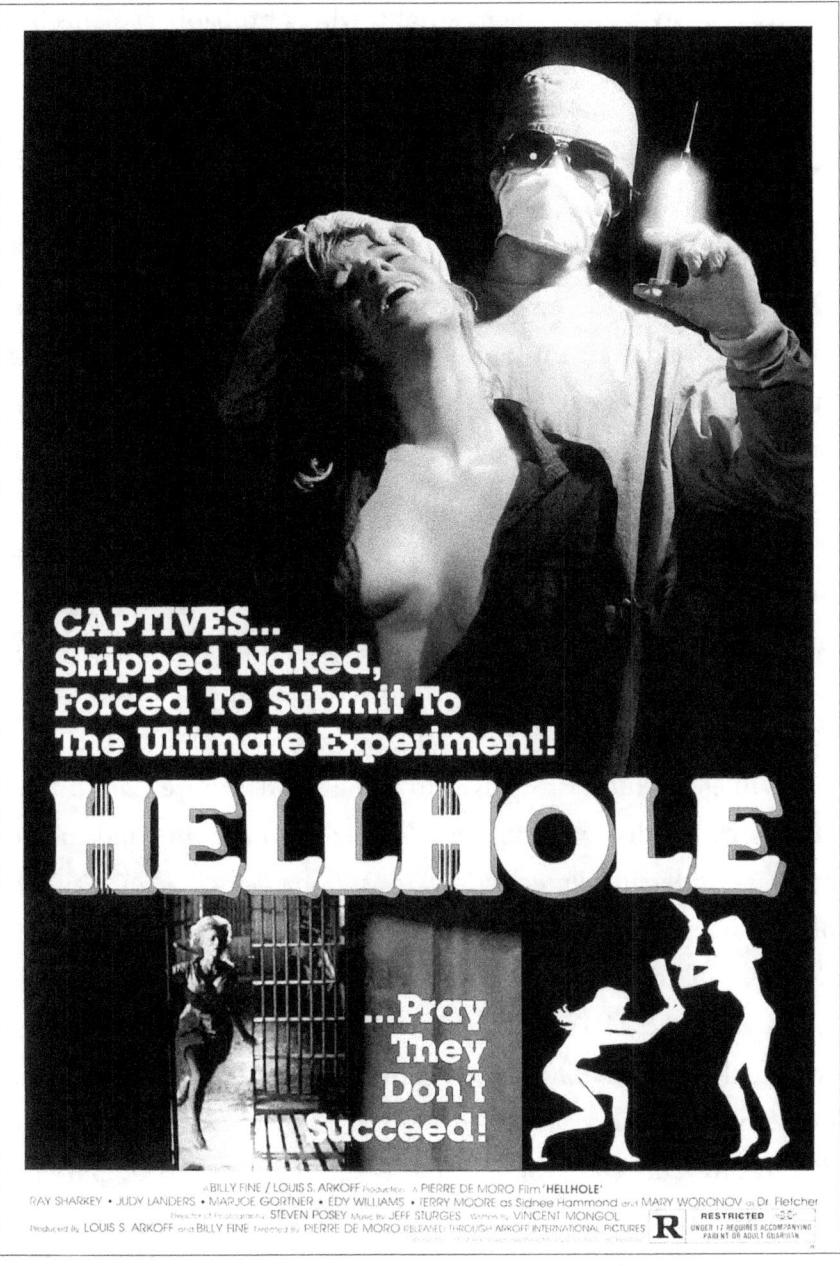

American one–sheet poster for *Hellhole*.

It's a shady establishment alright, which probably explains how such a clearly dubious character like Ray Sharkey's can land a job as an orderly at such ease. In one of the film's most memorable scenes, a disturbed young woman named Curry (Marneen Fields) is dragged off to the Hellhole after having some religious hallucinations and stomping her way across the tabletops in the mess hall. Once secured to the gurney in the Hellhole, helpless and dressed only in her light blue uniform skirt and white sneakers, Dr. Fletcher approaches and asks Curry what she is afraid of. "The Devil", she replies in stuttered fear. When Dr. Fletcher asks her who she thinks the Devil is, Curry replies: "You." We know poor Curry is doomed from that point, and after the latest attempt at a chemical lobotomy once again results in failure, she is given a painful death needle to the back of the neck, but even death does not bring any respite for her, as she is subjected to a postmortem kiss on the lips from the evil Dr. Fletcher.

While the lurid story is outrageous and a pure comic book fantasy for adults, what makes *Hellhole* so interesting and memorable is the terrifically eclectic cast assembled for it. You have the blonde television star (Judy Landers), the former child evangelist (Marjoe, of course), a Warhol actress and Roger Corman regular (the statuesque Mary Woronov), a notorious wild man and drug addict (the late Ray Sharkey), a former wife of legendary sexploitation filmmaker Russ Meyer (Edy Williams), the debut performance of a future cult star (the enormous–chinned Robert Z'Dar) and a genuine Hollywood glamour gal from the 1940s (Terry Moore from 1949's *Mighty Joe Young*). There's also Marneen Fields, whose performance as the doomed Curry drew praise and comparisons to Sissy Spacek from co–producer Louis Arkoff and the film's French director Pierre De Morro.

Third-billed in the film's opening credits, Marjoe's role in *Hellhole* is a fairly limited one and his Dr. Dane is more of a supporting character, though certainly a pivotal one, and his scenes alongside Fields and Woronov in the Hellhole are what help give the movie a large part of its *frisson* (shots from the scene also featured prominently in the film's original theatrical trailer). Dane's motivations in the movie are ambivalent—he and Dr. Fletcher are both equally complicit in the horrific experiments being conducted on inmates in the Hellhole, but while Dane tries to justify his participation in them from the view of valuable scientific research, Fletcher seems to be in purely to satisfy her own perverse sexual kinks. When Dane accuses Fletcher of using their experiments to compensate for sexual hang–ups, Fletcher replies by telling him: "At least I have sexual hang–ups. You don't even have sex." Next to the intimidating, statuesque form of Mary Woronov's Dr. Fletcher, Dr. Dane is impotent both authoritatively and sexually.

After a brief theatrical run, *Hellhole* fell into something of a distribution hellhole of its own. It received a VHS and laserdisc release in the 1980s, but in the ensuing years was available only from bootleg video and DVD sources. Fortunately, the movie was saved from obscurity in 2016 by Scream Factory, who released *Hellhole* on a double-disc Blu–ray/DVD set. Unfortunately, the original negative for the film was unavailable and is presumed lost, with Scream Factory having to piece the film together from a couple of different prints. The resultant transfer does have a little softness and graininess, as well as the odd scratch and emulsion mark, but this is the best the film is ever likely to look, and these little 'defects' do help preserve the grindhouse appeal of the film, without distracting from it one little bit.

Marneen Fields on Marjoe Gortner

A SAG actor since 1976 who studied professionally for eight years while forging a career as a pioneering Hollywood stuntwoman in films and on television since the mid–70s, Marneen Fields became the first actor to come from the professional stunt arena to be cast in a prominent acting role in a feature film, and her time onscreen in *Hellhole* is very memorable indeed, from the intense physicality she displays during her mess hall rampage with a look of genuine fear and religious fervor etched across her face, to the abject terror she is able to convey while she is strapped helplessly to the gurney in the Hellhole (not to mention an impressive display of her long hair being shaken wildly about during her reaction to the chemical lobotomy). Today, Fields continues to act and write screenplays, and under the name Marneen Lynne has established herself as an award-winning singer and songwriter.

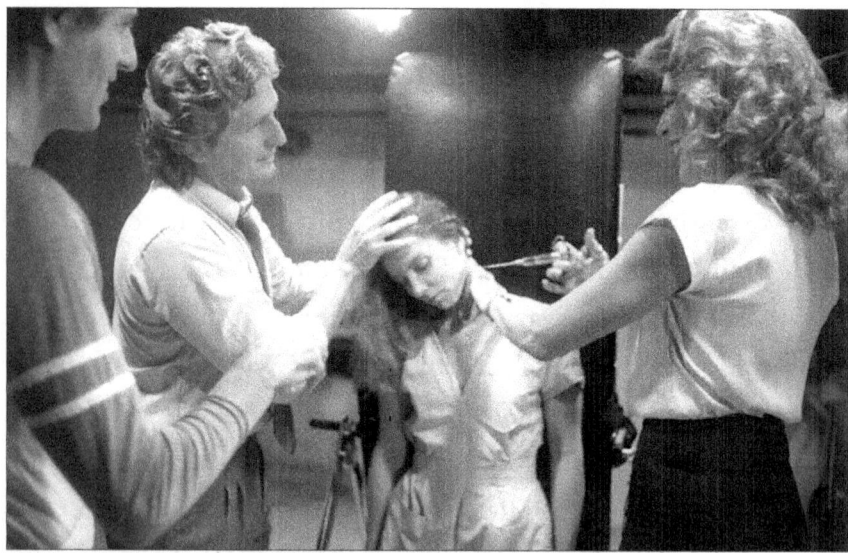

Behind the scenes shot of director Pierre De Moro (far left) going over the scene where Marneen Fields (center) as the doomed Curry receives a chemical lobotomy from Dr. Dane (Marjoe Gortner) and Dr. Fletcher (Mary Woronov) in *Hellhole*.

What was Marjoe like to work with?
Marjoe Gortner was wonderful to work with. He approached me after each of my performances in the scenes I appeared with him in, in *Hellhole* and gave personal critiques of my performances each time, always in a softly spoken and professional way.

Did you get to study or observe his acting techniques?
Yes, I did observe and study his acting techniques as he was a Hollywood legend. The one thing I can say about Marjoe's craft of acting in *Hellhole* is that his work is seamless, effortless and flawless and that's what makes him so amazing to watch.

I believe the first time you got to meet Marjoe was when he turned up on the set to film your scene in the Hellhole. What was your initial impression of him?
The first time I saw Marjoe was during the cafeteria scene in *Hellhole*. He was in character as Dr. Dane, and Mary Woronov was in character as Dr. Fletcher. We had already shot the first half of my cafeteria scene where I hallucinate that the Devil has poisoned the food and throw the inmates' plates of food off the tables, along with throwing one of the nurses who tries to contain me onto the floor. Then, I jump up onto the top of the long table, stepping into the plates of food as I make my way across the table to the end, where I jump up onto a counter, turn around and begin speaking in tongues. While I'm speaking in tongues, Dr. Dane, Dr. Fletcher and two orderlies enter the cafeteria to stop my outburst and cart me off to the Hellhole, where the two Drs. perform a chemical lobotomy on me. It was such a shock to me when I looked up and saw them because in my mind as I read the script and prepared for my role, I expected Dr. Fletcher to be an older and more stout

nurse, I never expected super model Mary Woronov to appear in the role. When the take was over I was surprised when I looked over and Marjoe was standing next to me, almost as if he had ran up to me. He pulled me aside and introduced himself. He was very nice as he told me in a polite way that a person doesn't speak in tongues like that, that he had been an evangelistic minister in life, and this is how it's done. He then proceeded to coach me speaking in tongues for a few seconds, showing me how it's done.

Did you find not having the chance to rehearse with him a hindrance or a help in terms of your own performance and getting into your character?
I did get a chance to rehearse with both Marjoe and Mary Woronov prior to shooting my scenes in *Hellhole*. In the cafeteria scene Marjoe wasn't in the scene with me, only Mary Woronov and the two orderlies.

I believe Marjoe had some nice words and feedback regarding your acting and performance?
Yes, I also appeared in the lengthy chemical lobotomy scene in *Hellhole*, performing my entire scene while strapped to a gurney and being tortured by Dr. Dane and Dr. Fletcher. Some of the scene took place with me alone in two-shot with Marjoe. After the chemical lobotomy scene was wrapped I realized Marjoe was standing close to me and pulling me aside. He whispered into my ear that I was really great in that scene. It meant so much to me that he liked my work in the scene and took time to give his critique once again, and complimented my work this time.

A few years after filming Hellhole, you caught up with Marjoe again at the Golden Boot Awards (a ceremony established by actor Pat Buttram which ran between 1983 and 2007 and acknowledged achievements in the western genre of movies and television). What was that experience like?

I ran into Marjoe a few times after the filming of *Hellhole*, once at the cast party at Louis Arkoff's house in Mulholland Canyon and again at the Golden Boot Awards. I also remember standing near him and his exquisite car one day outside one of the sound stages, I think during a *Hellhole* looping session. His car was golden or yellow and it was like a Ferrari or a Mercedes or something, definitely top of the line, looked brand new and may have had a sunroof. Hard to remember, so many years have gone by. I introduced myself and he remembered me. He told me he was with William Morris Agency and that he was producing. I was so thrilled to run into him also at the Golden Boot Awards one year, he was the best first–class country dressed man in the room as you can see in the photo. On that amazing evening, Clint Eastwood, Burt Reynolds, Lonnie Anderson and Jane Fonda were also in the room. I approached Marjoe who was attending the event with a woman with a brown bob haircut, they seemed quite close as he seemed to pay her a lot of attention. I introduced myself, once again he remembered me and smiled, and complimented me on my performance in *Hellhole*. He was just great when I asked him if I could get a photo with him. Once again, my memories of Marjoe are that of a wonderfully soft spoken and professional gentleman. His demeaner was very gentle, unassuming, polite and of strong character.

Marjoe Gortner in all his western finery catches up with his *Hellhole* co-star Marneen Fields at the 1993 Golden Boot Awards.

Luigi Cozzi, who directed Marjoe in Starcrash in 1979, told me that Marjoe was very close to Lou Arkoff, who produced Hellhole. Did you get the sense on set that there was an obvious closeness between them?

No, I would have never known they were close friends as they didn't seem to hang out together on the set and I never saw them spending a lot of time chatting. I did see Lou spend a lot of time discussing everything with director Pierre DeMoro. Louis Arkoff is a very hands–on producer and is as responsible as Pierre DeMoro and

Marjoe Gortner for my renown dramatic performance in *Hellhole* that's won me such great reviews and respect for my acting.

When did you first become aware of Marjoe past as a child preacher and evangelist? Did this change your perception of him at all?
As soon as I found out he was a child preacher and evangelist I adored him even more as a human being and remembered seeing him preach as a young girl and wondering how a child could be anointed in such a way. Marjoe Gortner has had an amazing calling in life and wonderful blessings of fame, fortune and success on so many levels. I admire him tremendously.

Dr. Dane (Marjoe Gortner) prepares a drugged Curry (Marneen Fields) for her terrifying treatment in *Hellhole.*

THE SURVIVALIST
USA/1987/93 minutes
Director: Sig Shore
Writer: John V. Kraft
Producers: David Greene & Steven Shore
Cast: Steve Railsback, Susan Blakely, Cliff De Young & Marjoe Gortner

Practiced primarily, or at least most famously, in the United States, survivalism as a movement had its origins as far back as the 1930s (spurred in part by the Great Depression following the 1929 Wall Street crash), but became more visible and widespread during the early Cold War period of the late–1940s and 50s, when American fear and paranoia over Russia having the atomic bomb was at its most intense. Children across the country were taught to "Duck and Cover" if they saw the atomic flash on the horizon, while their parents were busy building bomb shelters in their backyards and stockpiling them with water and canned goods. Survivalism continued into the 1970s thanks to the 1973 oil crisis, and in the 90s after President Clinton signed the (now–expired) Federal Assault Weapons Ban, and peaked over fears of what havoc the ticking of the clock into the year 2000 was likely to cause to the world's computer systems (as we all know, the world went on remarkably unaffected). Today, survivalism continues to be practiced by many, and was showcased on the popular reality series *Doomsday Preppers*, which first aired on the National Geographic Channel between 2011–2014.

Also known as *Jack Tillman: The Survivalist*, *The Survivalist* is an action adventure film straight out of the 1980s, inspired by a mix of histrionics over Ronald Reagan's "Star Wars" defense program, the popularity of *First Blood* (1982) and the subsequent rise of John Rambo as an iconic American hero. Unfortunately, it all adds up to a rather bland and unexciting ride, with very little in the way of tension or suspense, not to mention common sense.

When a nuclear explosion, triggered by an unknown source, detonates over an uninhabited area of Eastern Siberia, the United States is thrown into a panic when the USSR accuses America of being behind the attack. Fearing swift reprisals, the President declares a state of emergency and calls out the National Guard to quell any looting or panic in the streets. In Spring Wells, Texas, construction magnate Jack Tillman (Steve Railsback) is enjoying a barbeque with friends when news of the nuclear incident breaks. Not wanting to stand by and let the government take care of matters as the population quickly spirals out of control with riots and looting, Tillman loads up his armory and takes off to the local gas station to fill up his truck, where he has a run-in with Lieutenant Youngman (Marjoe Gortner), the motorbike-riding leader of the local National Guard, with whom Tillman has been having a bitter feud since their days in Vietnam together.

Returning home to find his wife and daughter have been raped and killed by looters (the neighborhood descends into total anarchy *really* fast in this movie), Tillman gathers up his best friend, Dr. Vincent Ryan (Cliff De Young) and his nurse wife Linda (Susan Blakely) and heads for the isolation and relative safety of the desert mountains, with Youngman in hot pursuit, determined to "make an example" of Tillman for making a mockery of the National Guard's authority. Youngman tells his patrol leader: "We're almost in a state of war, and we haven't got time to waste on looters and hoarders and patriotic scum like the men we are about to go after!"

Heading north in an attempt to find his young son Danny (Jason Healey), who was away on a school camp when martial law was introduced, Tillman and his companions have to deal with redneck county border cops and makeup-wearing biker gangs while staying one step ahead of Youngman and his hunting party. After the naïve Vincent breaks off on his own and is promptly killed by two hitchhikers he stops to pick-up, it isn't long before Tillman and Linda find time to bed down together, before they finally locate the almost-forgotten Danny, who has been sensibly hiding out in a cave (it seems the survivalist instinct are only instilled in the males of the Tillman clan). In what turns out to be a rather anti-climactic confrontation, Youngman conveniently catches up with Tillman just at the right time to take Danny hostage, though the Survivalist is in of course no mood to negotiate, taking care of Youngman with a well-thrown knife to the throat, followed by a burst of gunfire to the chest to finish him off.

Playing another National Guardsman as he did in *Earthquake*, Marjoe Gortner is robbed of all the little quirks that made his Jody character in that disaster movie so memorably odd, his Lt. Youngman being a fairly rigid and straight military type who enjoys the power his position enables him to wield. He is unfortunately given very little to do with his character other than walk around stiffly with a stern look on his face, barking orders and occasionally using his fists to break up fights between his men in order to show them who's boss. There's no real explanation for why so many National Guard resources are being used just to track down three lone renegades when the whole country seems to have descended into utter chaos, the sole motivation being the fact that Tillman humiliates Youngman by running over his bike with a tractor while he breaks into the local bank in order to retrieve his safety deposit box.

Certainly, one of the main assets of *The Survivalist* is in the casting of Steve Railsback in the title role. The Dallas-born Railsback first rose to prominence with his galvanizing performance as notorious cult leader Charles Manson in *Helter Skelter*, the two–part television mini-series which documented the vicious Tate–LaBianca murders that terrified Los Angeles, and shocked the rest of the world, during the latter part of 1969. Railsback followed up *Helter Skelter* with performances in Richard Rush's *The Stunt Man* (1980), the violent futuristic Australian prison drama *Turkey Shoot* (1982) and Tobe Hooper's crazed sci-fi/horror adventure *Lifeforce* (1985) before landing the role of Jack Tillman. So convincing was his performance as Manson that Railsback became somewhat typecast at playing slightly odd or nervous characters, which may have been unfair to such a fine actor but certainly made him a perfect choice to play Tillman. Railsback would later go on to play another infamous real–life figure when he portrayed the deranged Wisconsin farmer Ed Gein in *In the Light of the Moon* (aka *Ed Gein*, 2000).

The music for *The Survivalist* was composed by Tony Camillo and has a very 80s flavored synth/rock feel that's very typical of low–budget action films of the period, though it seems oddly out of place here. Camillio also helped write and produce some of the music for a couple of cult genre favorites in *The Toxic Avenger* (1984) and *Street Trash* (1987). *The Survivalist* was also the name of a long–running series of pulp paperback adventure novels, written by firearms expert Jerry Ahern and first published in the US in 1981. Though they shared similar themes, the film was not an official adaptation of the novels, though they clearly provided some degree of inspiration in it.

After working for some time as a distributor, Sig Shore didn't direct his first feature until 1975's musical drama *That's the Way of the World*, by which time he was already 56 (he had started dabbling in directing in the mid–1960s, helming a number of sporting shorts starring Norwegian ski racer—and Olympic gold medalist—Stein Eriksen). Shore would only direct a total of five features in his relatively short (1975–1990) directorial career, including the trashy female vigilante film *Sudden Death* (1985) and the belated 1990 Blaxploitation sequel *The Return of Superfly* (Sig Shore had been a producer on the first two *Super Fly* movies from 1972/73, and under the name of Mike Richards even played the part of the Deputy Commissioner in the original).

AMERICAN NINJA 3: BLOOD HUNT
USA/February 24, 1989/89 minutes
Director: Cedric Sundstrom
Writer: Gary Conway
Producers: Harry Alan Towers, John Stodel & Avi Lerner
Cast: Steve James, Michele Chan, Calvin Jung, Marjoe Gortner & David Bradley

Anyone who regularly rented videos during the 1980s would no doubt be familiar with the names Menahem Golan and Yoram Globus and their Cannon Films production company (a financially ailing company which Golan and Globus took over in 1979 and briefly revitalized). And even if those names don't ring a bell, chances are you have watched many of their films which they produced and distributed during that decade. While Cannon Films did finance and distribute some critically successful movies such as *Runaway Train* (1985) and *Barfly* (1987), and dabbled in the horror, fantasy, breakdance and softcore erotica genres, they were mostly known for their string of violent action and exploitation films like *Enter the Ninja* (1981), *Missing in Action* (1984), *The Delta Force* (1986) and three of the *Death Wish* sequels starring Charles Bronson. Though many of their films made money at the box office, Cannon found their biggest audience in the living room, where their movies proved to be perennially popular home video rentals.

Another of Cannon's popular hits was *American Ninja* (1985), a martial arts action film that was originally planned as a vehicle for Chuck Norris, who was then one of the biggest names on Cannon's roster of stars. When Norris passed on the project (supposedly because he didn't like the idea of having his face covered during many of the ninja sequences), Golan and Globus brought in a relatively unknown young American actor named Michael Dudikoff and immediately began to package him as their discovery and next big star. Dudikoff did have boyish good looks and some genuine screen charisma that was put to good use in *American Ninja*, and when Cannon were developing a (never–produced) Spider–Man film in the late–eighties, he was being publicly touted as their casting choice for the title role.

American Ninja proved popular and profitable enough to establish a brief franchise, with Dudikoff returning for *American Ninja 2: The Confrontation* in 1987, but by the time *American Ninja 3: Blood Hunt* came along two years later, the young star was gone, the once tight relationship between Golan and Globus had become strained to the point of breaking, and Cannon Films were feeling the financial pinch from investing in several big–budget productions which bombed at the box–office (a diversion from Cannon's previously successful business model of producing many lower–budget features and thriving on the profits of the films which did well, rather than producing less films but with bigger budgets).

Along with star Dudikoff, the names Golan and Globus are also absent from *American Ninja 3: Blood Hunt,* but one name which does return from the first two films in the series is Steve James, the late African American actor, martial artist and stuntman who had a charismatic screen presence that was put to good work in movies like William Lustig's *Vigilante* (1983), William Friedkin's stylish crime classic *To Live and Die in L.A.* (1985) and the blaxploitation spoof *I'm Gonna Git You Sucka* (1989). James receives top billing in *American Ninja 3: Blood Hunt,* reprising his role as Corporal Curtis Jackson, with former karate champion David Bradley replacing Michael Dudikoff as Sean Davidson, the new American Ninja. While Dudikoff's ninja was as an amnesiac street thug with extreme ninjitsu skills named Joe Armstrong who is conscripted into the US Army by a judge as an alternative to prison, Bradley's character comes from a more innocent and tragic background.

American Ninja 3: Blood Hunt opens up in 1979, with a prologue depicting Sean Davidson as a young boy (played by Stephen Webber), eagerly waiting for his father to make his entrance for the main event at a karate tournament. Unbeknownst to him, while his father (Eckard Rabe) is getting a rubdown in the change room, a brutal and mysterious terrorist known as The Cobra (Marjoe Gortner) and his henchmen are on their way to the stadium to rob the box–office. Predictably, both Sean and his father get caught up in the ensuing chaos, with dad getting shot and killed right in front of the young kid's eyes. Taking a leaf out of the classic origin story of The Batman (and many other comic book and pulp heroes), Sean uses the tragedy to spur him on to achieve mental and physical perfection, and he is taken under the wing of Master Izumo (Calvin Jung), who spends the next decade training the boy in the art of ninjutsu and guiding him through his journey into manhood.

Ten years later, Sean Davidson, now an adult in his mid–twenties and a fully trained ninja, finds himself on the remote Caribbean island of Triana, where he has been invited to compete in a mysterious martial arts tournament (a popular narrative ploy for martial arts cinema since it was used in the 1973 Bruce Lee classic *Enter the Dragon*). It is here that Davidson meets up with Curtis Jackson (Steve James) and Dexter (Evan J. Klisser), two fellow competitors who become fast friends and end up helping him when he uncovers the truth behind the tournament: that it has been set-up by The Cobra as a means to find the best physical specimen to use as a guinea pig for his germ warfare experiments. Naturally, Sean Davidson is the one ultimately selected to be The Cobra's test subject, and after getting shot–up with a dose of the villain's deadly serum, he faces a race against time as—aided by Jackson, Dexter and a female mistress of disguise (played by Michele B. Chan)—he tries to obtain the antidote, avenge his father and stop The Cobra from selling his weapon to the highest–bidding terrorist.

Publicity photo of Michele B. Chan and Marjoe Gortner in *American Ninja 3: Blood Hunt*.

Shot in South Africa on a budget that seems low even by Cannon standards, *American Ninja 3: Blood Hunt* is nonetheless a fun action/martial–arts film which director Cedric Sundstrom manages to imbue with a few interesting creative touches. The sequences that take place inside The Cobra's laboratory in particular have a colorful, comic book–esque design to them, their sparseness giving them the same sense of surreal minimalism as 1960s fantasy television shows like *Lost in Space* (1965–1968) and *Batman* (1966–1968). There's also some nice use of prosthetic makeup in the shots where Michele B. Chan's character reveals her disguise and deception skills, and prolific composer George S. Clinton caps off his soundtrack with a suitably silly but catchy commercial rock track called "The Cobra Strikes", performed with Lisa Kauppi, which plays over the final credits.

Unfortunately, Marjoe's role in *American Ninja 3: Blood Hunt* is a pretty one–note and thankless one. There is sadly very little about his character that resembles the venomous and lightning–quick reptile which he is named after. When he is confronted and cornered by the American Ninja at the film's climax, he basically crumbles and cowers in fear, and his last desperate lunge at Davidson is killed off by a swift round kick to the head. Still, Gortner does bring a nice effective smarminess to his character, much like a late–night cable TV salesperson who looks and sounds smooth but you know you just shouldn't trust, and he does show a sense of sartorial elegance, particularly in the opening 1979 prologue sequence, where he rides in the backseat of his car decked–out in a white suit and looking as if he is heading off for a spot of cocaine–fueled disco dancing at Studio 54.

One interesting name to be found amongst the credits on *American Ninja 3: Blood Hunt* is that of screenwriter Gary Conway, who started off his career as an actor, playing the titular role in

Herbert L. Strock's B–movie classic *I Was a Teenage Frankenstein* (1957) and is remembered by fans of classic television as Captain Steve Burton on Irwin Allen's *Land of the Giants* (1968–1970). Conway also wrote the original story for *Over the Top* (1987), the big–budget Sylvester Stallone vehicle whose commercial failure helped send Cannon Films into financial ruin, as well as the screenplay for *American Ninja 2: The Confrontation* (1987). His only other known writing credit is for the drama *Woman's Story* (2000), which he also directed and starred in.

Cedric Sundstrom on Marjoe Gortner

A South African born filmmaker of Swedish descent, Cedric Sundstrom started making 8mm shorts in his home country at a young age, before working as an assistant director on such productions as *Killer Force* (1976), *Zulu Dawn* (1979), *Safari 3000* (1980), as well as the Cannon Films productions *King Solomon's Mines* (1985) and its sequel *Allan Quartermain and the Lost City of Gold* (1986), and the space fantasy *Gor* (1987) and its follow–up *Outlaw of Gor* (1988). His features as a director include *Captive Rage* (1988), *The Revenger* (1990), *American Ninja 4: The Annihilation* (1990) and the true crime TV docudrama *The Suitcase Killers* (2002).

Do you recall how Marjoe would have been cast for the role of The Cobra in American Ninja 3? Was he the first choice for the role?

At the time I was heavily involved with the casting for a new American Ninja to replace Michael Dudikoff. My first thought for the Cobra was George Chakiras because I am a great fan of *West Side Story* (1961). I put the suggestion through to Don Pembroke—the casting director—who later came back with his own suggestion of Marjoe, and I jumped at it.

At the time, how familiar were you with Marjoe's past as a child evangelist? Was it something that you ever discussed with him, or something he ever talked about on set?

I was vaguely aware of his evangelical past. I had seen and was very impressed by *When You Comin' Back, Red Ryder*, but we never had any time during the shooting to discuss his past or mine.

What sort of working relationship did you have with Marjoe? Was there much collaboration and improvisation in his depiction of The Cobra, or did he play the role pretty much as written?

There was definitely a great deal of improv from Marjoe in his rounding out of his character, as I was rewriting the script with a new approach to reflect Marjoe's own attributes—such as his charm and high camp—which begged to be included. Therefore, the Cobra became more of an alluring proselytizing villain. I can say quite honestly that we had a lot of fun together.

I'm surprised Marjoe didn't do more work for Cannon Films during the mid-to-late 1980s, as he seemed like the sort of name and face that would have worked well within Cannon's roster of regulars.

I agree with you, but as you know there was only one other *American Ninja* film on the cards (*American Ninja 4: The Annihilation*), and the Cobra had met his fate in Part 3. He would have been a formidable villain for the future.

Did you stay in touch or have any further contact with Marjoe after the filming of American Ninja 3?

Unfortunately not, but who knows? He is still alive, and so am I.

FIRE, ICE & DYNAMITE
Germany/October 18, 1990/106 minutes
Director: Willy Bogner
Writer: Tony Williamson
Producers: Willy Bogner & Bernd Eichinger
Cast: Roger Moore, Simon Shepherd, Shari Belafonte, Marjoe Gortner & Uwe Ochsenknecht

Marjoe Gortner's penultimate film appearance (to date) was in this strange action/comedy/sports film that seems to be trying to ride far too late on the coattails of road race derby films like *The Gumball Rally* (1976) and *The Cannonball Run* (1981) and its sequels, only with soft white snow replacing hard grey asphalt. Roger Moore heads a rather eccentric cast as Sir George, a billionaire tycoon environmentalist with mounting debts who decides to fake his own death in order to watch over the running of the "Megathon", a special winter sports event set–up by Sir George to determine who will inherit his estate. Sir George's three illegitimate children, daughter Lucy (Connie De Groot) and sons Alexander (Simon Shepherd) and Dudley (Roger's son Geoffrey Moore), all born to different mothers, have to compete against their father's creditors to claim the $135 million left behind in his will.

Watched over by Sir George's Scottish butler McVay (billed as Rod Tailby but clearly Roger Moore in an obvious disguise and bad accent), the three potential heirs band together to form their own team to compete in the Megathon. Calling themselves "Fire and Ice" and helped by Sir George's personal assistant Serena (Shari Belafonte), we are treated to a comical stunt sequence depicting the flamboyant Alexander's attempt at learning to ski, as well as seeing some of their competitors own bumbling attempts to master certain activities like paragliding, before the Megathon proper finally begins. Starting off with some dry rock skiing down a mountain in the Pyrenees, the Megathon also includes such hair-raising challenges as scaling a sheer dam wall, bungee jumping from high bridges, riding the river rapids and speed skiing the snowy slopes (including some 360-degree loops). Naturally, despite some attempts at chicanery from rival teams, Fire and Ice end up winning the Megathon, saving Sir George's empire from his creditors and bringing his fragmented family closer together than they have ever been.

Marjoe Gortner's role in *Fire, Ice & Dynamite* is that of Dan Selby, a television sports anchorman working for the ISN network, who is at the Megathon to provide running commentary on the event and its individual challenges. Dressed in a burgundy winter sports suit with yellow trim, and often calling the action from a helicopter, Marjoe does pretty well in a limited role that is there clearly to help tie the individual segments together and keep some semblance of an organized competition going. Marjoe's earlier jobs as presenter on *Speak Up, America* (1980) and the *Circus of the Stars* TV specials (1979–1987) seem to have helped him out somewhat here, as he comes across with the energy and flair of a natural sports reporter, staying professional while also showing an enthusiasm and boyish excitement in his voice. And of course, he has that confident salesman smile.

Fire, Ice & Dynamite represents the closest Marjoe ever came to appearing in a James Bond movie (I always though Gortner would have been perfect for the role of Joe Butcher, the shonky televangelist and front for a drug smuggling operation, as played by entertainer Wayne Newton in the 1989 007 film *License to Kill*). Not only does *Fire, Ice & Dynamite* star the then-recently-ex-Bond Roger Moore, whose last time out in the role was in *A View to a Kill* (1985), but the director of the film, German-born Willy Bogner, had worked on a number of the Bond films himself, photographing the often hair-raising ski sequences for *On Her Majesty's Secret Service* (1969), *The Spy Who Loved Me* (1977), *For Your Eyes Only* (1981) and the aforementioned *A View to a Kill*. In fact, one of the ski stunts in *Fire, Ice & Dynamite*, involving skiers using outdoor picnic tables as landing pads and ramps, is very similar to a stunt in *For Your Eyes Only*, while the sequence of Sir George faking his own death by jumping out of his private plane without a parachute, only to be provided one in mid-air during on his descent, echoes the jaw-dropping freefall pre-credit sequence from another Roger Moore Bond film, *Moonraker* (1979).

Bogner's early career was as an alpine ski racer, competing in the 1960 Winter Olympics and achieving a fourth placing in the slalom at the 1966 World Championships before concentrating on his work as a cameraman. His initial experience as a filmmaker was a tragic one. While in Switzerland in April of 1964 to film scenes for what would be his first movie, *Ski Fascination* (1966), an avalanche struck and buried several members of the crew, killing Bogner's then-girlfriend Barbara Henneberger (an Olympic Bronze medalist) and American skier Wallace "Buddy" Werner. Bogner, initially tried and acquitted of homicide by negligence, was later convicted on appeal of manslaughter by negligence, though he only received a two-month suspended sentence. Bogner also began designing his own popular line of ski wear in the early-seventies, which Roger Moore can be seen wearing in the Bond movies, garnering the filmmaker/designer a nice commercial plug for his product.

Willy Bognar's previous film to *Fire, Ice & Dynamite* was simply called *Fire and Ice* (1986) and was more of a straightforward ski documentary, so it would seem his goal was to re-envision *Fire and Ice* as an action adventure movie, adding the *Dynamite* for some extra excitement and drama while still being able to capitalize on the exhilarating ski photography.

Apart from its leading characters, some of the unexpected faces which pop-up in *Fire, Ice & Dynamite*—most of them playing themselves—include astronaut Buzz Aldrin, champion Formula 1 driver Niki Lauder, America's Cup yachting captain Dennis Conner and tennis ace Steffi Graff, who injured her thumb while filming a skiing sequence and had to be sidelined from the tennis courts for several weeks as a result. Just as eclectic as the cast is its soundtrack, which was released in Germany on the Ariola label and includes the hard rocking title track performed by Deep Purple alongside cuts from Bonnie Tyler and cast members Isaac Hayes ("Fly") and Jennifer Rush ("We Are the Strong"). The sleeve of the soundtrack release features the same nice piece of art used on the film's theatrical poster, which was painted by Italian artist Renato Casaro and features a nice winter action collage that once again recalls the Bond films of the 1980s. Casaro himself had previously painted the international posters for 007 movies like *Octopussy* (1983) and the rogue Sean Connery installment *Never Say Never Again* (1983), as well such other movies as *Conan the Barbarian* (1982), *Dune* (1984), *Rambo: First Blood Part II* and *Army of Darkness* (1992).

Narratively wafer-thin and boasting visual gags that elicit more groans than guffaws, *Fire, Ice & Dynamite* nonetheless amply achieves what Bognar no doubt set-out to do, delivering an often visually spectacular ode to the thrill of the daredevil, and clearly having a lot of fun while doing so. Some of the hair-raising stunts captured here by cinematographer Charly Steinberger are quite impressive and would look particularly exhilarating on an IMAX screen I would imagine.

Renato Casaro's promotional poster art for *Fire, Ice & Dynamite*.

WILD BILL

USA/December1, 1995/98 minutes
Director: Walter Hill
Writer: Walter Hill
Producers: Richard D. Zanuck & Lili Fini Zanuck
Cast: Jeff Bridges, Ellen Barkin, John Hurt, Diane Lane, Keith Carradine, David Arquette, Christina Applegate, Bruce Dern & Marjoe Gortner

"To the very end, he embraced his fate."

In *Wild Bill*, Marjoe Gortner brings his career full circle by playing a brief cameo role as a preacher in this western character study written and directed by Walter Hill, whose directorial credits include such cult films as *The Warriors* (1979), *The Long Riders* (1980), *48 Hours* (1983) and *Streets of Fire* (1984), as well as being an uncredited screenwriter on *Alien*.

Starring Jeff Bridges in the title role, *Wild Bill* documents the final days in the life of James Butler "Wild Bill" Hickok, the legendary 19th Century lawman, gunfighter and gambler of the old American West. Beginning with his burial and intercut with black & white flashbacks to his younger days, the bulk of the film takes place after Bill arrives in Deadwood in the Territory of Dakota, a fearsome reputation behind him but struggling with not only the ghosts of his past but failing eyesight caused by glaucoma. While he reflects on his life and the world which is changing around him (helped by the opium which he obtains from the local Chinese immigrants), Wild Bill renews his friendship with old flame Calamity Jane (Ellen Barkin) and has to deal with a young upstart named Jack McCall (Davis Arquette) who has come to town to settle the score with Bill for deserting and breaking the heart of his mother Susanna (Diane Lane), ironically the only woman he ever really loved. Realizing he can't outsmart (or outdraw) Bill on his own, and after an attempt to pay some gunslingers to take care of his problem on his behalf fails, McCall ends up sending Hickok to his grave at age 39 with a cowardly bullet in the back, delivered while Bill is sitting at the card table holding an aces and eights, which would thereafter become famous as the Dead Man's Hand.

Billed simply as "Preacher", Marjoe's one scene in *Wild Bill* arrives at the half–way point of the film, as Bill strolls in from the rain to watch Gortner's character exalting his love for the Lord and the Bible to a small group of true believers (and maybe a few people hoping to cleanse their souls of guilt).

> *"Well hallelujah, let's lift up our hands tonight and praise the Lord. Let's praise him, hallelujah! Hallelujah, how I love the Lord! I love Him, because He is able. I love Him, because He reached down and He pulled me right from the gutters of sin. I love Him, because when sin and sickness had me bound, He reached out, He washed me in His precious blood."*

As Bill stands in the doorway watching the preacher send his audience into possessed rapture, it triggers a flashback to the night he met Susanna, a memory which quickly has him racing back to the Chinese part of town to seek solace in the opium pipe.

Written by Hill and based on two separate books (*Deadwood* by Pete Dexter and *Father and Sons* by Thomas Babe), *Wild Bill* combines both fact and fiction and the story is brought to life by a terrific cast that also includes John Hurt (whose English character Charley Prince narrates the film), Diane Lane, Keith Carradine as Buffalo Bill, Bruce Dern, James Remar (so good as Ajax in *The Warriors*) and Christina Applegate.

Unfortunately, Marjoe's final film (to date) did not prove to be a box–office winner, with the $30 million production struggling to earn just over two million dollars during its brief run in nearly 800 American cinemas. While the 90s were not a huge decade for westerns, movies like the Oscar–winning duo *Dances with Wolves* (1990) and *Unforgiven* (1992), along with *Tombstone* (1993) still managed to find large audiences, making the commercial failure of *Wild Bill* rather disappointing considering the depth of talent involved in the production. Hill expressed disappointment in the way Allied Artists promoted the film, believing it mislead audience expectations into what they were going to see. It's far from a classic of the western genre but it certainly doesn't deserve the almost total obscurity it has languished in since its release. Powered by a typically impressive performance by Bridges, the film is a baroque and melancholy ode to a period of American history which has long since passed into mythology.

CHAPTER FOUR

Marjoe on the Groove Tube: Television Appearances

A NOTE ABOUT the television listings: Entries are listed chronologically according to the original US air date of the first episode in the series. Dates listed for individual episodes represent the original US air date for that particular episode. Running times listed are for the original airings with commercials included.

MEDICAL CENTER
USA/CBS, 1969 – 1976/171 episodes/60 minutes each
Regular cast: James Daly, Chad Everett & Audrey Totter
Episode: "Demi-God", Season 6, Episode 2, 16 September, 1974

Marjoe Gortner seemed tailor made for his guest–starring role in this popular and long–running medical drama series set in an unnamed university health complex in Los Angeles. In "Demi-God", he plays David, a faith–healer whose wife Paulina (Meredith Baxter) is stricken with cancer, leaving the poor woman torn between seeking professional medical treatment or trusting in her husband's ability to heal by faith and the force of will.

Marjoe Gortner being interviewed by showbiz reporter Army Archerd at the December 16, 1976, premiere of the Peter Bogdanovich film *Nickelodeon*.

ABC'S WIDE WORLD OF ENTERTAINMENT
USA/ABC, 1973 – 1975/22 episodes/90 minutes each
Episode: "Marjoe's Country: Nashville", Episode 3, 16 July, 1973

An early attempt to sell Marjoe's natural charm and personality to a television audience came via this rare special, in which Gortner takes viewers on a tour of some of the highlights of Nashville and its surrounding areas, including a livestock sale in Murfreesboro and interviews with country music artists Hank Snow ("The Yodeling Ranger") and Ernest Tubb ("The Texas Troubadour"). One of Hank Snow's tracks, "Four in the Morning", written by Jerry Chesnut, was later featured on the soundtrack to *When You Comin' Back, Red Ryder.*

Marjoe's Country: Nashville was part of a series of late-night specials packaged by ABC to go up against the NBC ratings juggernaut that was *The Tonight Show* with Johnny Carson. *ABC's Wide World of Entertainment* featured specials on subjects as diverse as Phyllis Diller, The Un-Official Miss Las Vegas Showgirl Pageant, James Dean and the Kennedy assassination. The Marjoe Nashville special was co-produced by Desilu Productions and directed by Arthur Forrest and Bill Jersey, the later of whom received an Oscar nomination for co-directing the race relations documentary *A Time for Burning* (1967).

POLICE STORY
USA/NBC, 1973–1978/103 episodes/60 minutes each
Creator: Joseph Wambaugh
Episodes:
"Requiem for an Informer", Season 1, Episode 2, 9 October, 1973
"War Games", Season 2, Episode 20, 4 March, 1975

One of the most highly regarded police drama series' of the 1970s, *Police Story* was created by former cop Joseph Wambaugh, who after 14 years with the LAPD turned his hand to writing both fiction and non-fiction crime-based novels (*The New Centurions, The Choirboys, The Onion Field* and *The Glitter Dome* were amongst his better-known works, all of which were adapted into films of decent quality). *Police Story*, which Wambaugh based on his own experiences within the police force, was told in an anthology format, with each episode featuring a completely different cast of actors and leading characters (though there were a few exceptions), making it in effect more like a collection of self-contained short films than the standard episodic cop show. Character driven and filled with great, tough dialogue, *Police Story* was an admirably gritty and realistic series which made great use of a fine roster of performers, writers and directors throughout its six seasons and 103 episodes. The use of police radio chatter as a voice-over to start most episodes gave the series a quasi-documentary tone that helped heighten the drama and tension and pull you in. And much like real life, a lot of the tales told in *Police Story* ended on a matter-of-fact, low-key note rather than the clichéd shoot-'em-up climax.

Marjoe Gortner made two appearances on *Police Story*, the first and most noteworthy one coming in the second episode of the show's first season. "Requiem for an Informer" was written by Sy Salkowitz and directed by Marvin Chomsky, and has Marjoe top-billed as Stan, a junkie who turns police informer in order to stay out of jail on a bank robbery charge. Cops Tony Calabrese (Tony Lo Bianco) and Bert Jameson (Don Meredith) put Stan to work on the streets, trying to uncover information on a team of violent serial bank robbers who have moved their operation to L.A. after terrorizing Seattle. As Stan feeds them information that eventually lead the cops to the leader of the robbery ring (played by the wonderfully deep-voiced Michael Ansara), Calabrese slowly develops an affection for his troubled informant, buying him new clothes to help him find a proper job and encouraging him to quit the junk for good and fly straight. Unfortunately, as the title of the episode tends to blatantly give away, poor Stan doesn't get the chance to repay Calabrese's faith in him, succumbing to his addiction and dying of a heroin overdose as the episode ends and the two cops arrive to deliver the good news about the busting of the robbery gang.

While Calabrese is genuinely upset and angry by Stan's death, his partner's biggest concern is who they are going to recruit as their next informant.

Looking particularly youthful and boyish, not to mention as thin as he's ever been, Marjoe delivers a terrific performance in "Requiem for an Informer." As in *The Marcus–Nelson Murders* earlier the same year, he excels at playing a strung-out street denizen, but his character in "Requiem for an Informer" is a lot more sympathetic and tragic, and Marjoe uses some nice subtleties to help his character endear himself to the audience without seeming forced or melodramatic. Stan is not overly bright, but he is intrinsically well-meaning and harmless. He wants to do the right thing but is a slave to his addiction. Like Calabrese, we are rooting for Stan to get his life together and make something of himself, which makes his death seem even more of a tragic waste, even though we aren't surprised at the eventual outcome. Marjoe plays off well with Tony Lo Bianco, who was still riding on the success of a couple of great performances in *The Honeymoon Killers* (1970) and *The French Connection* (1971). The duo of Lo Bianco's Calabrese and Don Meredith's Bert Jameson would provide *Police Story* with two of its few recurring characters, the pair eventually appearing in four episodes together along with some solo appearances.

Also appearing alongside Marjoe in "Requiem for an Informer" are Sharon Farrell as Bobbie and Mews (aka Mayra) Small as Shirley, two women who have taken pity on Stan and offer him a few dollars to perform odd jobs around their apartments. Mews Small had an interesting and rather eclectic acting career, with film appearances in Woody Allen's *Sleeper* (1973), *One Flew Over the Cuckoo's Nest* (1975), *Thank God it's Friday* (1978), the underrated fan stalker slasher *Fade to Black* (1980), Ralph Bakshi's animated *American Pop*

(1981) and the hit teen sex comedy *Zapped!* (1982). Her TV work included a role as a masseuse on "The Ripper" episode of *Kolchak: The Night Stalker* (1974–1975).

Marjoe's second and final appearance on *Police Story* came in the "War Games" episode from late in the show's second season. This time, as Detective Earl Gordy, he gets to play a character on the other side of the law, as Gordy and his partner Jack Ballard (Michael Parks) go undercover to infiltrate a white supremist gun club run ruled over by wealthy racist arms dealer Bud Ellwood (Murray Hamilton). To work his way up towards Ellwood, Gordy first has to win the trust of seedy gun store owner Norman Schoeler (Neville Brandt) and his group of redneck buddies, who sit around swilling beer and discussing the various preferred ways of killing black people (at one point even plotting to drive through a black part of town blasting away on a machine gun that they have anchored to the back of a station wagon).

When Gordy and Ballard finally get to meet Ellwood at a rambunctious barbeque on his estate, the arms kingpin is initially wary of the pair (especially Ballard, whom Ellwood accuses of having the stink of police all over him), but in a test of their faith he recruits the pair to carry out a hit on an influential Jewish political fundraiser who is both sympathetic to black issues and loudly critical of gun rights. Just to make sure he rubs salt into the wound, Ellwood insists that the assassination be carried out with a German firearm, and a note stating "Revoke Fair Housing" be nailed to his forehead! So rampant is Ellwood's paranoia that when Gordy and Ballard eventually reveal themselves to be cops, he initially disbelieves them, accusing them instead of being rivals out to kill him and take off with his gun stash. Unfortunately for Ellwood, a climactic machine gun shoot–out leaves him lying dead at the base of his own private target range.

The themes presented in "War Games" are quite confrontational and its subject matter is perhaps even more relevant today than it was in 1975. Certainly, the topics of gun ownership and the legal availability of semi–automatic weapons are more hotly debated than ever in the tragic wake of seemingly endless mass shooting incidents, particularly across the United States. Meanwhile, the NRA (National Rifle Association) continues to yield so much power and influence that most high–ranking politicians seem reluctant to take them on. In "War Games", most of the gun advocates are depicted as little more than racist, beer–guzzling yahoos who no doubt treat their weapons better than they do their wives, and of course it's this primitive simplicity which helps make them all the more frightening. Even more intimidating are those at the head of the snake, like Bud Ellwood, because they have the money, influence and thin veneer of respectability to actually spread their hatred and act upon their violent thoughts in more grand and surreptitious ways.

Along with its provocative dialogue, one of the most disturbing moments in "War Games" occurs at the barbeque thrown by Bud Ellwood, where several of his drunken gun nut followers take turns shooting at life–size wooden cut-outs of "a black, a hippie and a commie–pinko" (in the words of Schoeler), the frenzy culminating with Gordy literally shooting the head off the cut–out of the black man when called upon to prove his marksmanship. It's a scary scene, like a barbeque from Hell, made even more intimidating by the familiar defiant cries of being a legitimate gun club which neither the neighbors nor the authorities can do anything about ("I'd give my life for a 50–caliber machine gun right now", says a black cop through gritted teeth as he watches the scene unfold from his hidden vantage point).

"War Games" also presents Marjoe Gortner with one of his best characters and he really gives a nicely nuanced performance as Earl Gordy. Though he has the look and attitude needed to make his undercover act convincing, inside he is clearly sickened by the work he is doing and by the people he is required to associate and integrate with. Gordy's only real tenuous connection to the outside world are the brief clandestine phone calls he is able to have with his wife and young daughter, the later of whom is clearly too young to understand why her father needs to be away for such long periods of time, and hoping that he will be able to make her big school dance recital that's coming up (of course, in true television fashion Gordy makes the recital just in time to see his daughter take to the floor).

Along with Marjoe, there is a very strong roster of names at work in "War Games." Anyone who is a fan of Tobe Hooper's strange Texan swamp horror *Eaten Alive* (aka *Death Trap* aka *Starlight Slaughter* aka *Horror Hotel*, 1977) will know how memorably crazed Neville Brandt can be, and his craggy features, stringy hair and nervy, sweaty persona certainly helps bring an element of true revulsion to his character of Norman Schoeler. Those who swarm around Schoeler at his gun shop are likewise played by hardened, intimidating faces like Mills Watson and John Quade, while Murray Hamilton imbues Bud Ellwood with a skin-crawling, slimy suaveness. With his distinctive voice and thick pomp of greying hair, Hamilton often had the look and demeanor of a shonky loan shark or used car salesman, an attitude which served him well in what is no doubt the best known role from his long career, that of Mayor Larry Vaughn in *Jaws* (1976) and its sequel *Jaws 2* (1978), a character whose ignorance and concern over loss of tourist dollars indirectly resulted in the deaths of several people in the water.

Fans of 1980s grindhouse cinema will enjoy seeing a young Robert Ginty, who would play the title character in the violent

42nd Street grindhouse favorite *The Exterminator* (1980), show up in an early role as an acquaintance of Schoeler who comes into his store to sell him a box of stolen combat fatigues (heightening Gordy's fears that the gun group are planning an act of violence). Playing Gordy's concerned and lonely wife Pam, Brooke Bundy was a familiar face who turned up in a long list of television shows going back to *The Donna Reed Show* in 1962. By the 80s she was appearing in exploitation and horror fare like *Mission Kill* (1986), *Stewardess School* (1986) and *Beverly Hills Bodysnatchers* (1989). She also played the character of Elaine Parker in *A Nightmare on Elm Street 3: Dream Warriors* (1987) and *A Nightmare on Elm Street 4: The Dream Master* (1988).

BARNABY JONES
USA/CBS, 1973–1980/178 episodes/60 minutes each
Created by: Edward Hume
Regular cast: Buddy Ebsen & Lee Meriwether
Episode: "A Gold Record for Murder", Season 2, Episode 18, 10 February, 1974

One of a number of popular and long-running shows that were produced in the 1970s by Quinn Martin, *Barnaby Jones* starred Buddy Ebsen as a retired detective who goes back to work after his son (who had taken over the detective agency) is murdered while investigating a case. After solving his son's murder, Jones decides to return to detective work full-time, enlisting the help of his widowed daughter-in-law Betty Jones (Lee Merriweather, who starred in the Irwin Allen fantasy TV series *The Time Tunnel* and played Catwoman in the 1966 *Batman* movie).

Barnaby Jones differentiated itself from many of the other detective shows of the time by having a leading star that was somewhat older than usual (Ebsen was 65 at the time the series premiered in 1973). The series proved quite popular thanks primarily to its unique angle and the likeable and somewhat quirky performance of Ebsen in the title role (he was of course best known as Jed Clampett in *The Beverly Hillbillies* television series of the 1960s). *Barnaby Jones* would eventually run for eight seasons and 178 episodes.

Marjoe Gortner appeared in a single episode of *Barnaby Jones* from the show's second season. In "A Gold Record for Murder" he plays David Colton, a young rock star clearly on the rise, driving a flash car and performing a regular gig to enthusiastic crowds at the famous Gazzari's nightclub on Sunset Strip. But the pressure is on from his manager and record label to deliver new songs to keep the momentum going, songs which Colton just doesn't have in him. In fact, while Colton may be a charismatic singer and stage performer his songwriting skills are a fraud, and he has been paying young composer and lyricist Raymond Walding (Michael Zaslow) to write his material and pass it off as his own. But when Walding starts demanding the proper credit for his latest work, Colton kills his ghost songwriter by spiking his coffee with a lethal overdose of heroin which he had picked up from his supplier following the gig earlier in the evening. Now the burgeoning superstar has not only cut off the source for his future material, but has to deal with Barnaby Jones sticking his beak in, after Raymond's mother hires the detective to dig deeper into her son's death, not convinced that he would have taken heroin willingly.

While spouting the usual clichés about rock musicians and their thirst for drugs and trouble, Barnaby Jones happens to spot a David Colton album with a promo stamp on it while sifting through Walding's record collection, leading him to make the most tenuous of connections between the victim and the rock star. With a new album due in two weeks and Jones sniffing at his tail, Colton's troubles increase when his manager learns the truth about Colton's phony songwriting and his involvement in Walding's death, a problem which the increasingly on–edge singer, desperate to preserve his reputation and critical respect, solves with a well–aimed bullet. Barnaby Jones eventually lands a connection between Colton and a unique drug pouch that belonged to him which was found at the scene of Walding's fatal overdose. The inevitable showdown takes place, appropriately enough, at the recording studio that Colton is working in, with Barnaby seemingly familiar enough with studio recording soundboards to use them to distract Colton with loud music long enough to put a slug in his stomach. Though it looks like Colton has bought the farm as the scene fades out, the epilogue lets us know that he not only survived the shooting but confessed to the two murders, thereby clearing Raymond Walding's reputation and tying things up in the traditionally neat television knot.

There is a lot of great moments involving Marjoe in "A Gold Record for Murder", which help make it one of the actor's real television high points. Gortner plays the cocky young rock star to the hilt as he delivers through his golden smirk lines like this, delivered to Barnaby Jones during their first encounter: "You don't look like a groupie, so what can I do for you? And don't try to tell me it's my fault that your granddaughter ran away from home." Later, he vents his frustration to Jones about his limitations: "You can't just be a singer anymore, not with these kids. You gotta be a creator, a damn poet!"

You have to wonder if Marjoe was enjoying his David Colton character as a way to live out a taste of the success he was hoping to achieve in the music industry when he released his only solo musical LP, *Bad But Not Evil*, in 1972. In fact, one of the songs from that album, Marjoe's great rockin' cover of the 1971 Jethro Tull song "Wind Up" is used for a sequence where Colton is rehearsing one of his new (stolen) songs for an upcoming recording session. The opening scene showing Colton strutting his stuff on stage is also marvelous, with Marjoe decked out in tight gold pants and blue eyeshadow dominating his face as he belts out a raucous number called "Where Are You Hiding?", a Stones–like bluesy rocker with an Alice Cooper flavor to the vocals. Colton's band can also be seen behind him, all wearing various degrees of exaggerated facial makeup. The look and Style of Colton is clearly inspired by the big glam rock stars of the day, in particular Cooper and David Bowie, though offstage he looks more like a typical West Coast rock musician trying out for a spot in The Eagles. Sadly the episode does not contain any specific information or credits regarding the music used in the show, so the origins of "Where Are You Hiding?" are tough to pinpoint.

Other interesting names that show up in "A Gold Record for Murder" include Meg Foster from *The Todd Killings* (1971), *Guyana Tragedy: The Story of Jim Jones* (1980) and John Carpenter's *They Live* (1988), and Jason Evers, who under the name Herb Evers starred in the classic (and very sleazy) low–budget horror film *The Brain that Wouldn't Die* (filmed in 1959 but not released until 1962). The episode was directed by George McCowan, who apart from numerous TV shows also helmed the fun nature-strikes-back AIP film *Frogs*, as well as the sci-fi misfire *The Shape of Things to Come* (1979), which was inspired more by *Star Wars* than the classic H. G. Wells novel it claimed to be based on.

NAKIA

USA/ABC, 1974/13 episodes/60 minutes each
Created by: Michael Butler & Christopher Trumbo
Regular cast: Robert Forster, Arthur Kennedy, Gloria DeHaven, Taylor Lacher & John Tenorio, Jr.
Episode: "The Moving Target", Season 1, Episode 8, 9 November, 1974

A short–lived cop series which only lasted one season and is sadly rarely-seen today, *Nakia* starred the charismatic Robert Forster as Nakia Parker, a police officer from the Navajo tribe on duty in New Mexico and trying to do his job in the face of injustice towards his fellow Native Americans (an injustice that often stems from the people he works with). The flight of the Native American was very much a prominent social issue of the decade, and had been tackled successfully on screen in Tom Laughlin's independent action/drama hit *Billy Jack* (1971), while genre films from later in the 70s like *Nightwing* (1979) and *Prophecy* (1979) also focused on Native American characters and themes as part of their narrative.

In "The Moving Target", Nakia and his nephew Half Cup (John Tenorio, Jr.) are enjoying a spot of fishing when the officer confiscates a rifle from a stranger named Cal Terman (John Bennett Perry), who is conducting target practice on forbidden land. When he discovers that Terman is an ex–con who is not allowed to possess firearms, Nakia tracks him to Albuquerque, where he suspects Terman is gunning for a former friend, a singer named Sonny Streeter (Marjoe Gortner), who is headlining a folk music festival there.

Also guest starring alongside Marjoe in "The Moving Target" is Robin Mattson, a young actress who had appeared with Tiffany Bolling in the seedy grindhouse favorite *Bonnie's Kids* (1972), and appeared in a lot of TV movies and episodic shows before landing her biggest role as Gina on the daytime soap *Santa Barbara*

(1984–1993), a character she played for over a thousand episodes between 1991–1993.

ARCHER
USA/NBC, 1975/6 episodes/60 minutes each
Developed by: David Karp
Regular cast: Brian Keith & John P. Ryan
Episode: "The Turkish Connection", Season 1, Episode 1, 30 January, 1975

Another short–lived crime drama. Based on a fictional character created by American–Canadian writer Ross Macdonald in 1949, and first portrayed onscreen (though with a different surname) by Paul Newman in *Harper* (1966) and *The Drowning Pool* (1975). For this small screen incarnation, Brian Keith plays Lew Archer, a former cop now a private detective working L.A. Clearly meant as an homage to the classic film noir and hard–boiled detective pulp stories of the 1940s, *Archer* simply did not click with viewers and was cancelled by NBC after only two of its six episodes were aired. Macdonald's 1971 novel *The Underground Man* was also unsuccessfully developed as TV pilot in 1974, with Peter Graves in the lead role of Lew Archer.

In the debut episode of *Archer*, "The Turkish Connection", Marjoe Gortner guest stars as Rick Faust, the editor of an underground newspaper who agrees to go undercover for Archer in order to help break up an extortion ring. The episode was directed by Gary Nelson, whose few ventures out of TV land include the big–budget Disney sci–fi adventure *The Black Hole* and *Allan Quartermain and the Lost City of Gold* for Cannon Films.

LAUGH-IN
USA/NBC, 1977–1978/6 episodes/60 minutes each
Created by: George Schlatter
Regular cast: Robin Williams, Ben Powers, Kim Braden, June Gable & Sergio Aragonés

Perhaps the most iconic and enduring pop satire of its day, the original run of *Rowan & Martin's Laugh-In* lasted from 1968 until 1973, a five-year run that produced 140 hour-long episodes for NBC (which were later re-cut into 30-minute shows for syndication). Tackling everything from sex and race to politics and religion, not to mention the hotly-debated Vietnam War, *Laugh-In*'s rapid-fire assault of sight gags, jokes and musical numbers made it seem as if the "usual gang of idiots" from *MAD Magazine* had taken over *The Ed Sullivan Show*. It was the highest-rating show in its timeslot during the second and third seasons, featured a roster of big-name guest stars and was vital in helping to launch the careers of Goldie Hawn, Lily Tomlin and others.

When NBC decided to resurrect the show in 1977, after four years off the air, they did so by leaving the names of Dan Rowan and Dick Martin off the title, incurring the legal wrath of the original show's hosts, who still owned a percentage of the *Laugh-In* name and successfully sued the show's producer and creator George Schlatter for using the format which they had helped popularize without their permission. When the new show went to air towards the end of 1977, with a completely new cast and crew of writers, it was clear that not only was the magic missing but times had rapidly changed, and the new *Laugh-In* could not even hope to capture even a sliver of the pop culture zeitgeist as the original had done. It only lasted six episodes, and is most noteworthy today for showcasing some early work from Robin Williams, who was a regular cast member and appeared in all episodes. When Williams became a household name the following year thanks to his Mork from Ork persona on *Happy Days* (1974–1984) and his own *Mork & Mindy* (1978–1982) over at ABC, NBC cashed-in by rerunning the *Laugh-In* episodes as a series of summer specials in 1979.

Marjoe Gortner may not be the sort of person one would immediately think of when it comes to the style of humor embraced by *Laugh–In*, but then that was a big part of the appeal of the original show. It brought people out of their comfort zone and even managed to get the gruff and tough John Wayne to parade around in a fluffy bright lavender bunny suit for a 1969 episode. Though they were working which much weaker material, the list of guest stars who appeared during the short run of the new *Laugh–In* was still quite impressive, and included names like Bette Davis, Frank Sinatra, Roger Moore, Sonny Bono, James Garner, Henry Fonda, Tina Turner, Shirley MacLaine and others. Other than Williams, the most interesting name amongst the show's team of regular performers would have to be Sergio Aragonés, the Spanish cartoonist famous for his work on *MAD Magazine*, who both provided animation for *Laugh–In* as well as appearing in some of the skits.

Marjoe appeared as a guest on the fourth and sixth episodes of the retooled *Laugh–In*, but its scarcity even amongst collectors makes it hard to obtain or see today. Some of the Robin Williams skits from the show are available on You Tube but the rest remains frustratingly difficult to see and was unfortunately not included amongst the special features on the massive 38-disc *Rowan & Martin's Laugh-In: The Complete Series* box set released by Time Life/Wea in 2018.

BROADWAY ON SHOWTIME
USA/SHOWTIME, 1979–1980/6 episodes/90 minutes
Episode: "The Robber Bridegroom", Episode 5, June, 1980

Unfortunately, very little information is known about *Broadway on Showtime*, a short–lived series of specials put together for the then–fledgling Showtime cable network, which had been officially launched on July 1, 1976. As suggested by its title, *Broadway on Showtime* featured filmed adaptations of Broadway plays. Marjoe Gortner starred in the fifth installment in the series, playing the role of Jamie Lockhart in an adaptation of Alfred Uhry and Robert Waldman's *The Robber Bridegroom*, a musical which had first run on Broadway in 1975.

Based on a Grimm fairy tale–inspired 1942 novella by Southern author Eudora Welty, the bawdy, innuendo–laden stage version of *The Robber Bridegroom* took place in 18th-century Mississippi and was a riff on the Robin Hood legend, with Jamie Lockhart appearing to be an honest, law–abiding man whom is welcomed into the home of wealthy plantation owner Clement Musgrove after Lockhart saves him from a group of robbers. But Lockhart harbors a secret identity, that of The Bandit of the Woods, smothering his face with berry juice (!) to disguise his face. Set to a backdrop of bluegrass–inspired songs and music, Lockhart has to deal with the amorous advances of Musgrove's wife Salome, but his daughter Rosamund as well, who has fallen in love with Lockhart's villainous alter–ego.

While some episodes of *Broadway on Showtime* were filmed as live performances straight from the stage, *The Robber's Bridegroom* was videotaped on studio sets without an audience.

Sadly, while he certainly puts in an earnest and eager performance, the dual role of Jamie Lockhart and The Bandit of the Woods seems to be a bit much for Marjoe to get a handle or a nice balance on, especially within the harsh confines of the theatrical setting. He was filling some big shoes, stepping into a role that Raul Julia, Kevin Kline and Barry Bostwick had made big impressions with on stage (Bostwick in particular, winning himself a Tony Award for Best Performance by a Leading Actor in a Musical in 1976). Nonetheless, it's a good example of Marjoe's willingness to tackle a variety of genres in an attempt to expand his repertoire and avoid being pigeonholed.

FANTASY ISLAND
USA/ABC, 1977–1984/152 episodes/60 minutes each
Creator: Gene Levitt
Regular cast: Riccardo Montalban, Herve Villechaize & Wendy Schaal
Episodes:
"Loving Strangers/Something Borrowed, Something Blue...", Season 4, Episode 15, 14 February, 1981
"Revenge of the Forgotten/Charo", Season 6, Episode 14, 19 February, 1983

Created by Gene Levitt and debuting on the ABC network on January 14, 1977, *Fantasy Island* was a weekly television series that built its popularity on a pleasing mix of drama, action, comedy and romance, and two memorable male leads in charismatic Mexican actor Ricardo Montalban as Mr. Roarke, the mysterious host and overseer of the titular holiday resort island, and Hervé Villechaize as his diminutive assistant Tattoo. Living up to its title, the show was pure fantasy and escapism, as each week a small planeload of new visitors would arrive on the beautiful, exotic island to indulge in and live out their most secret fantasies, which usually revolved around romance or wealth, along with the odd dose of revenge and the supernatural. While things predictably worked out well in the end for most of the visitors, the journey along the way was never as predicted, and the show built itself around the "be careful what you wish for" idiom. *Fantasy Island* would eventually run for 152 episodes over seven seasons.

Marjoe Gortner made two guest appearances on *Fantasy Island*. In the fourth season story "Something Borrowed, Something Blue...", Marjoe plays Nick Corbin, a suave and menacing pimp who tries to blackmail Pamela Archer (Shelley Smith), a former high-class hooker now desperate to hide her past from her prominent future husband, Governor Jack Foster (John Gavin). It's interesting to see some hints of Marjoe's Teddy character from *When You Comin' Back, Red Ryder* emerge in his performance here (it's also amusing to see him getting flung through a window by the seemingly supernatural strength of Mr. Roarke).

Gortner booked a return trip to *Fantasy Island* for the sixth season episode "Revenge of the Forgotten", this time playing Lorin Robertson, an ex-con who believes there is treasure buried somewhere on the island. Guest starring alongside Marjoe in this episode are Van Johnson, Nancy Kulp (best known as Jane Hathaway on *The Beverly Hillbilies*), Steve Kanaly and the legendary Spanish entertainer Charo!

CIRCUS OF THE STARS
USA/CBS, 1977–1994/19 episodes/60 minutes each
Producer: Bob Stivers

An annual television event that ran for 19 episodes, *Circus of the Stars* was a reality show that seemed inspired by the likes of *Battle of the Network Stars*, which had debuted on the ABC network in 1976. The concept behind *Circus of the Stars* was an obvious and simple one: take a range of celebrities (mostly from current

TV shows as well as a few movie stars past their prime) and watch them try their hand at performing various circus acts and routines. Amongst the roster of celebrities who appeared on the show throughout its lifespan were such diverse names as Lucille Ball, Scott Baio, Peter Fonda, Hulk Hogan, Dick Clark, Vincent Price, Telly Savalas, William Shatner, Leslie Nielsen and O.J. Simpson. Some episodes were filmed on location in places like Disneyland and Caesars Palace in Las Vegas,

Marjoe Gortner, with his looks and physique and sense of daring–do seemed a natural choice for *Circus of the Stars*, and he proved popular and appealing enough to warrant four appearances on the show, on its 4th (1979), 5th (1980), 6th (1981), 7th (1982) and 12th (1987) installments. Unfortunately, the series has never been released on home video and while a couple of full episodes can be found online, along with a number of shorter segment clips, footage of Marjoe's appearances on *Circus of the Stars* are difficult to find.

SPEAK UP, AMERICA
USA/NBC, 1980/60 minutes each

Speak Up, America was a short–lived news/current affairs/lifestyle program hosted by Marjoe Gortner alongside Rhonda Bates and former Miss Ohio Jayne Kennedy, who received an Emmy nomination for her work on the series covering American soldiers stationed in the Demilitarized Zone in South Korea. Filmed in front of a studio audience and delivered with a light–hearted, even comedic edge, some of the topics covered on *Speak Up, America* included male strippers, teenage drinking, gigolos, chemical dumping grounds and political conventions. "The stars are YOU", ran the promotional blurbs for *Speak Up, America*, which unsuccessfully tried to recreate the winning formula of the much more popular *Real People* series, which also ran on the NBC network from 1979 to 1983. Reruns of *Speak Up, America* aired in the US in the early–eighties but since then has faded into obscurity and episodes impossible to track down.

FALCON CREST
USA/CBS, 1981–1990/227 episodes/60 minutes each
Creator: Earl Hammer, Jr.
Regular cast: Jane Wyman, Robert Foxworth, Susan Sullivan & Lorenzo Lamas

Created by Earl Hammer, Jr. (who had enjoyed huge success in the 1970s with *The Waltons*), *Falcon Crest* was a prime–time soap which followed a template that had been made popular by shows like *Dallas, Knots Landing* (1979–1993), *Dynasty* and *Flamingo Road* (1980–1982). The lavish lifestyles of the mega–wealthy, and the inevitable dramas, scandals and tragedies that consume them, was something which middle–class audiences were drawn to in droves during the extravagant eighties. Bitchiness, boozing, blackmail, power struggles, mansions, illicit affairs, big hair and even bigger shoulder pads dominated these nighttime US soap operas, which gave audiences the wish fulfillment escapism they sought, along with an abundant of characters to despise.

Falcon Crest wasn't quite as big as *Dallas* or *Dynasty*, but it proved popular enough to last nine seasons and 227 episodes. Set within the titular California vineyard in fictional Tuscany Valley, the series centered on a heated battle over family fortunes, fought between iron–fisted wine matriarch Angela Channing (Jane Wyman) and her nephew Chase Gioberti (Robert Foxworth), who returns to Falcon Crest to claim his share of the inheritance after his father dies in a fall at the winery.

Marjoe Gortner landed one of the most visible television roles of his career when he was cast as slick storefront psychic Vince Karlotti for the sixth season of *Falcon Crest*, portraying the character in 17 episodes that originally aired from November 1986 to May 1987. Karlotti was yet again a role for Marjoe which couldn't help but echo back to his preaching days, using charm and words and a welcoming grin to win over unlucky–in–love Emma Channing (Margaret Ladd), who visits Karlotti in a desperate attempt to contact the spirit of her deceased fiancé Dwayne Cooley (Daniel Greene), who was killed in an earthquake (the type of outlandish scenario that wasn't rare to find in these nighttime soapies). Of course, Emma soon starts to forget all about poor Dwayne and falls under the spell of the phony mystic, who formulates a plan to take advantage of her broken heart (and bulging purse) for his own gains. Also taking advantage of Emma's infatuation with Karlotti is her hunky nephew Lance Cumson (Lorenzo Lamas), who uncovers the mystic's FBI record for bilking lonely ladies out of their life savings and blackmails him into encouraging Emma to hand over her stocks in a family–owned newspaper to him rather than her mother, Angela Channing.

The storyline gets even stranger, with Emma soon convincing Karlotti to make love to her while he has the spirit of Dwayne inside of him, and soon she is announcing their engagement to the press, much to the obvious discomfort of Karlotti. It soon becomes obvious why he is trying to avoid publicity: in the middle of the big wedding, the proceedings are interrupted by a trio of women who all claim to be still married to Karlotti! Understandably shocked by the revelation, Emma collapses at the altar while Karlotti high–tails it out of the church

Sporting a tiny rat's tail, Marjoe injects a lot of fun into the proceedings in *Falcon Crest*, helping to set his scenes apart from the show's myriad of storylines, which dealt with more traditional themes that you would usually expect from a series such as this. The sequence in the season's thirteenth episode, "Missed Connections", where Emma and Karlotti consummate their physical relationship in his tacky parlor is particularly amusing. Portrayed as a sweet but gullible airhead, Emma Channing is in her forties but acts like a ditzy schoolgirl with a weird (and potentially mean and violent) streak, and is still treated and controlled like an irresponsible child by her mother. There's an innocent charm to Margaret Ladd's performance as Emma, making her one of the few characters in the show which you can really care about.

T. J. HOOKER

USA/ABC, 1982–1985 & CBS, 1985–1986/91 episodes/60 minutes each
Creator: Rick Husky
Regular cast: William Shatner, Heather Locklear, Adrian Zmed & James Darren
Episodes:
"Slay Ride", Season 3, Episode 12, 17 December, 1983
"Lag Time", Season 4, Episode 21, 23 March, 1985

While he had worked steadily throughout the seventies, both in films and on television, *T. J. Hooker* gave William Shatner his first hit TV series lead since the cancellation of *Star Trek* in 1969. Shatner played Detective Sergeant Thomas Jefferson "T.J." Hooker, a no–nonsense plainclothes veteran who, in an attempt to tackle crime from its grass roots, bumps himself back to the life of a uniformed beat cop after his partner is murdered. Hooker's regular squad included three officers, Vince Romano (Adrian Zmed), Stacey Sheridan (Heather Locklear in her star–making role) and Jim Corrigan (former teen idol James Darren).

The first of Marjoe Gortner's two appearances on *T. J. Hooker* came in the third season's Christmas episode, "Slay Ride." Written by the show's creator, Rick Husky, the storyline sees Hooker going undercover as Santa Claus to stake out a Christmas tree lot where a big drug buy is rumored to be going down. Unfortunately, the bust quickly goes south when a young couple in a station wagon get in the middle of things and allow Marino (Marjoe), one of the crims Hooker was hoping to apprehend in the act, to escape. The young couple, Troy Eldridge (Robert Dryer) and his wife Sue Anne (Philece Sampler), who have a newborn baby and are struggling to survive, are soon revealed to be associates of Marino and are planning another heist together. As luck would have it, Officer Stacey Sheridan is in the local grocery store when Troy and Sue Anne hold it up at gunpoint and shoot the clerk, the young cop recognizing the couple as the same people who had foiled the earlier bust attempt, an incident that was brushed off at the time as a frustrating but genuine piece of bad luck.

While Hooker and Romano peruse a strip joint and question a dancer who is dressed as a scanty Santa Claus, Marino and the Eldridges sit holed-up in a dive motel, the tensions between them exacerbated by the continual cries of the newborn baby, which Marino and Troy demand that Sue Anne hand over so they can dump the poor child on the church doorstep and proceed unhindered with their crime spree. But having sacrificed her baby proves too much for Sue Anne, who snaps and takes off in her car, leaving an enraged Marino and her husband abandoned in the midst of a robbery attempt. Sue Anne of course heads straight back to the church where the baby had been dumped, and where Sheridan is now taking a personal interest in its wellbeing. With Marino and Troy close behind, followed quickly by Hooker and his team, a tense stand-off at the church ends with Troy shot and wounded,

Sue Anne safely in custody and Marino racing through some hilly suburban streets in his tan station wagon with Hooker in hot pursuit. After a reasonably solid TV car chase, Marino ends up rolling his wagon down a ditch, where he is pulled out by Hooker, shaken and stirred but still alive.

The main highlight of "Slay Ride" is seeing Marjoe act alongside Robert Dryer, a tall and rather menacing looking actor who became somewhat typecast playing violent or sadistic creeps, and for good reason—he was great at it. While his credits came mostly via episodic TV shows, a memorable feature film performance for Dryer was as Jake, head of a gang of vicious thugs who incur the wrath of the tight–clothed, crossbow-wielding Linda Blair in Danny Steinmann's rape–revenge classic *Savage Streets* (1984).

In contrast to Dryer's crazed psychotic demeanor, Marjoe comes across as your standard TV show thug, his Marino character made memorable mostly by his cigar–chomping and the colorful jacket he wears throughout the episode, which seems to reflect some bold Native American design.

Marjoe ran afoul of Hooker once again in the fourth season episode "Lag Time", now playing Jack Lewis, an ex–con living with Officer Romano's law school teacher Cynthia Randolph (Lauren Tewes) and the mastermind behind a spate of recent armed robberies. While Cynthia is aware of Jack's past, she is convinced he is flying straight and seems happy to help support him while he writes his memoirs. But when a security guard is killed by Jack during his crew's latest hold–up and Hooker comes knocking on Cynthia's door looking for him, the jig is up and Jack starts bringing out the firepower and threatening his girl with harm unless she agrees to drive the getaway car in the gang's next job. Marjoe's character doesn't get off as easily as in his first *T. J. Hooker* appearance, as Jack is shot dead by Officer Sheridan after being cornered in a warehouse following the expected post-bank job car chase (the climax also helps tie–up a subplot where Sheridan has been doubting her ability to be an effective cop after having a gun pointed in her face and only being moments from death).

MATT HOUSTON
USA/ABC, 1982–1985/67 episodes/60 minutes each
Creator: Lawrence Gordon
Regular cast: Lee Horsley, Pamela Hensley & George Wyner
Episode: "The Secret Admirer", season 2, Episode 20, 9 March, 1984

The prolific Aaron Spelling strikes again with yet another formulaic detective series firmly crafted from the *Magnum P.I.* mold, with Lee Horsley cast as the mustachioed title character, a filthy rich Texas oil tycoon who seems to have more than enough spare time on his hands to operate his own private investigation business while out in Los Angeles watching over his oil company's offshore drilling. Pamela Hensley played his attractive lawyer sidekick C.J. Parsons, and George Wyner his long–suffering business manager. The second season episode "The Secret Admirer" casts Marjoe Gortner in the guest star role of Christian Dean, a psycho stalker who is obsessed with C.J. and murders her boyfriend then threatens to kill her after she rejects his advances. As luck (and television convenience) has it, Matt Houston is out of town on business while most of the events go down, leaving poor C.J. to deal with the situation on her own.

THE A-TEAM
USA/NBC, 1983–1987/98 episodes/60 minutes each
Creators: Frank Lupo & Stephen J. Cannell
Regular cast: George Peppard, Dirk Benedict, Dwight Schultz & Mr. T
Episode: "Recipe for Heavy Bread", Season 2, Episode 2, 27 September, 1983

One of the most popular television shows of its day, *The A-Team* was an action adventure series which thrived on over-the-top stunts and witty wisecracks, as well as capitalizing on the position which the Vietnam War was starting to occupy within American pop culture, and the fascination with the survivalist mentality that was being popularized by movies like *First Blood*.

Created by Frank Lupo and Stephen J, Cannell, the premise of *The A-Team* has a group of Vietnam vets, members of a Special Forces unit, who escape from military prison after being court-martialed "for a crime they didn't commit" (according to the opening narration that is spoken by the show's producer, actor John Ashley). While on the run, they work as soldiers of fortune while waiting for the chance to be able to clear their names. Comprising the team were: Colonel John "Hannibal" Smith (George Peppard), Arthur Telmpleton "Faceman" Peck (Dirk Benedict), H.M. "Howling Mad" Murdoch (Dwight Schultz) and Bosco Albert "B. A." (Bad Attitude) Baracus (Mr, T). While Peppard received top billing, it was Mr. T who emerged as the show's true star, his mohawk, massive gold chain-adorned physique, sneer and "I pity the fool" catchphrase making him especially popular with kids and he remains an enduring icon of 80s Americana.

In the early second season episode "Recipe for Heavy Bread", Marjoe Gortner finds himself in familiar TV guest star territory, playing Tom Anderson, a former POW camp rat now importing

Chinese heroin into the United States with the help of his former camp commander, the vicious General Chow (John Fujioka). The A-Team become involved when they are sitting in a restaurant and miraculously recognize the chef as a Vietnamese camp cook who took pity on them and slipped them food when they were also prisoners of Chow. Now Chow wants revenge against the cook for his actions, but he and Anderson will have to deal with the A-Team if they want to get their hands on him.

While lots of bullets fly on *The A–Team*, people rarely die, and the end of the episode sees Anderson and ten–million–dollars–worth of his heroin locked inside a van and left by the A–Team to be found and properly dealt with by the cops.

HOTEL
USA/ABC, 1983 – 1988/114 episodes/60 minutes each
Created by: Aaron Spelling
Regular cast: Anne Baxter, James Brolin, Connie Sellecca & Shari Belafonte
Episode: "Images", Season 2, Episode 19, 3 April, 1985

Based on a 1965 novel by Arthur Hailey (the author of *Airport*), *Hotel* was another prime time drama series produced by Aaron Spelling that followed *Dynasty* on ABC and ran for five seasons, though it does not seem to be particularly well remembered despite nice production values and a regular cast that included Anne Baxter, James Brolin and Connie Sellecca, the later fresh off the just–cancelled former hit series *The Greatest American Hero* (1981–1983). Set within the elegant (and fictitious) St. Gregory Hotel in San Francisco, the series provided the perfect location for both the principal cast to get involved in drama, office politics and romantic liaisons, while a roster of revolving tenants at the hotel kept the subplots fresh and provided ample roles for familiar faces to guest star. Among that stream of faces was Marjoe Gortner, who in the second season episode "Images" plays one Frank Brenner, a hood who turns up at the St. Gregory to claim back his ex-wife Cathy (Donna Pescow), the hotel's new bookkeeper living in fear under an assumed name after testifying against the Mafia in a high-profile mob trial. The storyline of "Images" is very similar to the *Fantasy Island* episode "Something Borrowed, Something Blue...", which Marjoe guest-starred in. Further indication that he was clearly envisioned for specific roles by television heads, that of the charismatic but corruptive villain, and also proof of just how recycled the screenplays for episodic television can be. Donna Pescow, who plays Cathy in "Images" and is best known for her role as John Travolta's rejected dance partner in *Saturday Night Fever* (1977), would check-in to *Hotel* three times during the series' run, each time as a different character.

WHIZ KIDS
USA/CBS, 1983–1984/18 episodes/60 minutes each
Creator: Philip DeGuere & Bob Shayne
Regular Cast: Matthew Laborteaux, Todd Porter, Andrea Elson, Melanie Gaffin & Max Gail
Episode: "Return of the Big Rocker", Season 1, Episode 7, 23 November, 1983

Produced at a time when home computers, and home computer games, were still very much a new and novel thing, *Whiz Kids* centered on a group of four young high-school kids who use their expertise with computer technology to help local reporter Llewellen Farley (Max Gail) and police Lieutenant Neal Quinn (A Martinez) solve crimes happening around the local L.A. area. The initial idea for the concept had the four Whiz Kids performing a lot of borderline illegal or morally ambiguous tricks with their computer skills, particularly in terms of hacking and accessing personal records, so the reporter and lieutenant characters were brought in to provide a degree of guidance and supervision for the kids, placating the network and the show's sponsors who had shown concern over a potential negative image being portrayed.

In "Return of the Big Rocker", Marjoe guest-stars as Bobby Lee Janz, a rock & roll star who, at the height of his fame in 1963, was forced to fake his own plane crash death in order to avoid the wrath of a feared Vegas mob boss, who had put out a contract on Bobby for stealing, and later marrying, his favorite girl. Twenty years later, Bobby turns up under the name Bobby Dean singing 50s rock & roll in a San Fernando Valley dive bar called The Blue Bamboo, just as an unscrupulous record label is about to release an LP of phony recordings supposedly recorded by Bobby in Memphis just before his presumed death. When Farley catches Bobby's act and is instantly suspicious of how much he looks and sounds like the "late" Bobby Lee Janz, he enlists the help of the Whiz Kids to perform a computerized voice analysis which proves that Janz and Bobby Dean are one in the same. The Kids and Bobby end up becoming fast friends and are soon teaming up to rescue Farley, who is being held and subjected to sound torture in one of the studios of Nascorp Records, after Farley confronted the label boss about the faking of the lost Bobby Dean recordings.

Whiz Kids was clearly aimed at a young teen audience of squeaky–clean *Tiger Beat* readers, not to mention budding young computer geeks. While the concept behind the series seems noticeably influenced by John Badham's hugely enjoyable teen techno thriller *WarGames* (1983), co-creator Philip DeGuere maintained that the idea for *Whiz Kids* was first developed in 1981. The show certainly does have a nice charm in its innocence, a big part of which can be put down to the actors playing the four likeable Whiz Kids: Matthew Laborteaux (already a minor teen idol thanks to *Little House on the Prairie* and relentless promotion by *16 Magazine*), Todd Porter, Jeffrey Jacquet and Andrea Elson (who would go on to find much bigger success as Lynn Tanner on TV's *ALF*).

Marjoe Gortner seems to be having a lot of fun with his role as Bobby Lee Janz/Bobby Dean, enjoying the lighter tone and getting to belt out songs like "Great Balls of Fire", "When a Man Loves a Woman" and "Old Time Rock and Roll" while pounding away at his piano in a mock imitation of Jerry Lee Lewis. The backstory of Bobby Lee Janz being presumed dead in a 1963 light plane crash was clearly inspired by the real–life tragic deaths of Buddy Holly, Ritchie Valens and The Big Bopper on February 3, 1959, and the episode begins with a faux K-Tel style television commercial for the "lost" Bobby Lee Janz album, comprising of a selection of black & white photos of Marjoe in classic rock and roll and doo–wop poses.

Apart from the two Bobbys, Gortner ostensibly plays a third character in "Return of the Big Rocker" when he dons a fake moustache, white suit and Stetson and poses as music manager Hank Norman in order to gain access to the Nascorp Records studios. It's an amusing scene, with the Whiz Kids posing as Norman's band, an electronica outfit who call themselves The Computer Games (Depeche Mode, they ain't). The scene ends with the Whiz Kids and Bobby escaping the record label henchmen by chanting "Punk is Junk, Heavy Metal Rules!", sparking an in–studio fight between a group of punks and a heavy metal band (the former looking like A Flock of Seagulls rejects, the later a cross between Motley Crue and Spinal Tap).

Despite its timely subject and garnering five nominations at the 1983 Youth in Film Awards (a nomination for each of the four main actors and one for Best New Television Series), along with a cross-over appearance on the hot detective series *Simon & Simon* (another Philip DeGuere creation), *Whiz Kids* did not create much of a dent in its original Wednesday night spot and was cancelled after eighteen episodes. It remains relatively unknown today, and unavailable on home video other than a 2016 French DVD release.

AIRWOLF

USA/CBS, 1984–1986 & USA, 1987/80 episodes/60 minutes each
Creator: Donald P. Bellisario
Regular cast: Jan-Michael Vincent, Ernest Borgnine, Alex Cord & Jean Bruce Scott
Episode: "Dambreakers", Season 2, Episode 19, 16 March, 1985

Yet another action fantasy series, *Airwolf* took its clear inspiration from the John Badham film *Blue Thunder* (1983), starring Roy Scheider and Warren Oates as test pilots for a new high-tech experimental police helicopter. In *Airwolf*, Jan-Michael Vincent plays Stringfellow Hawke, a renegade pilot who makes a deal with a mysterious intelligence agency known as "The Firm" to fly an advanced military helicopter into dangerous situations. In exchange, Hawke is able to use the agency's equipment and resources to try and locate his brother, thought to be long-lost within the dangerous jungles of Vietnam.

In the second season episode "Dambreakers", Marjoe Gortner is once again cast in a role that echoed his real-life past, playing a character known as Brother Jebediah, leader of a religious commune with an anti-technology, back-to-nature philosophy whom Hawke is saddled with flying female reporter Kelly Dayton

(Heather McNair) out to interview. Arriving not via Airwolf but by regular copter, the duo quickly sense an atmosphere of tension within the supposed peaceful community, and Brother Jebediah is soon revealed to be one Johann Rector, a German-born extremist who is trying to free imprisoned members of his organization by committing acts of terror. While Rector's partner and second-in-command Hana (Devon Ericson) is worried that her leader is getting lost within his Brother Jebediah persona, Hawk and Dayton uncover a plot by the terrorist to bomb a nearby dam using an old World War Two-era B-25 Mitchell bomber, which they find hidden under a camouflage net while snooping around at night.

Caught and held capture in the commune, Rector reveals his plans to Hawke and Dayton and insists that the photographer will be there on the B-52 when the bombing takes place, in order to capture the big event on camera, with Hawke coming along for the ride. Not only will the bombing of the dam put more pressure on the government to cave-in to Rector's demands, but the resultant flood of water will tear right through the valley where many of the innocent followers seduced by the terrorist's Brother Jebediah charade have settled.

Fortunately, Hawke's father figure and mentor, pilot Dominic Santini (Ernest Borgnine) becomes worried by the sudden cease in communication from both Hawke and Dayton, and after procrastinating long enough to build tension until the last minute, wheels the Airwolf out of the hangar and whips it into action. Hawke and Dayton meanwhile manage to free themselves, but aren't able to stop Rector and Hana from taking off in the B-25. After Santini arrives and hands over the reins of the Airwolf to Hawke, it's up to the top whirlybird gun to hunt down the B-25 and bring it down with some well-aimed air-to-air missiles before it can release its deadly payload against the dam wall.

While it was a typically generic action/adventure series overall, *Airwolf* certainly delivered its fair share of dumb fun, and "Dambreakers" is one of the most enjoyable episodes and a definite highlight of the show's second season. The screenplay by Westbrook Claridge and Alfonse Ruggiero reflects some of the more notorious events involving cults and movements from the previous decade, including the kidnapping of Patty Hearst by the Symbionese Liberation Army in 1974 and the Peoples Temple religious group led by the Reverend Jim Jones, who forced over 900 of his followers to commit suicide in the steaming jungles of Guyana in November of 1978. The angle of terrified commune member Sara Longwood (Cindi Eyman) approaching Hawke and Dayton and asking them for help parallels those followers of Jim Jones who approached visiting American reporters and secretly passed them notes begging for help in getting away from the stifling and abusive ruling hand of Jones (it was this incident which helped spark the mass suicide along with the shooting of reporters and US Congressman Leo Ryan at a small jungle airstrip).

It's interesting to see Marjoe playing a dual role in "Dambreakers", with the Bible-spouting Brother Jebediah a character created to mask the true person within, Johann Rector, and his evil intentions (though like most extremists Rector believes there is just cause in his violence). You could almost read it as a sly commentary on Marjoe's real-life duality, the showy evangelist-turned-actor and the thin blurry line which often separated them. Gortner really delivers a fine solid performance here, relishing his dual roles and taking Rector over the top (I love the shots of him in the front machine gun dome of the stationary B-25 as he manically sprays the airport with bullets!) while channeling his own past as Brother Jebediah. It's easily one of the best television guest roles of his career.

There is also a refreshing emphasis on the female characters in this episode of *Airwolf*, and an enjoyable sense of war adventure, with the B–25 and dam bombing sequences clearly styled after Michael Anderson's *The Dam Busters* (1955), the classic British film which dramatized the famous bombing of German dams during World War Two, using a revolutionary bouncing bomb designed by Barnes Wallis. For the attack sequence on the dam, stock footage from Guy Hamilton's *Force 10 from Navarone* (1978) was used. There is also some dizzying and rather spectacular aerial shots captured of the Airwolf in action over the desert. Another asset to this episode is the synthesizer–driven score by Israeli composer Udi Harpaz, which accompanies the action and helps build the tension nicely (the show's main theme is also a great piece of pumping 80s synth). Director Virgil W. Vogel had been an editor of the Universal sci–fi classic *This Island Earth* (1955) and Orson Welles' masterpiece *Touch of Evil* (1958), and had directed the horror films *The Mole People* (1956) and *Invasion of the Animal People* (1959), before moving into television directing in the sixties, helming episodes of a long list of series including *Wagon Train* (1957–1965), *Bonanza* (1959–1973), *Mission: Impossible* (1966–1973), *The Streets of San Francisco*, *Miami Vice* (1984–1990) and many others.

OTHERWORLD
USA/CBS, 1985/8 episodes/60 minutes each
Creator: Roderick Taylor
Regular cast: Sam Groom, Gretchen Corbett, Tony O'Dell, Jonna Lee, Brandon Crane, Chris Herbert & Jonathan Banks
Episode: "Village of the Motorpigs", Season 1, Episode 5, 23 February, 1985

> *"Other worlds lie outside our seeing. Beyond the beyond. At the edge . . . of within. The Great Pyramid: erected by the Ancient Ones as a barricade. At the portal between two dimensions, two separate realities. This is the story of one family, drawn through a mysterious vortex into the other world—and of their perilous trek homeward."*

Otherworld was a strange science–fiction/fantasy series created by Roderick Taylor that ran for only eight episodes on the CBS network. The bizarre, trippy concept of the show could almost be described as a sort of *Lost in (Inner) Space*, with the plot revolving around an average American family (the Sterlings) who embark on a tour inside the Great Pyramid of Giza in Egypt, coincidently at the same time that the planets in our solar system align in a once–every–ten–thousand–years configuration which results in the family being transported to another planet called Thel which exists in some strange parallel dimension. Though Thel is inhabited by humans, it is split up into individual zones rather than countries, with each zone being individually governed and travel between zones strictly regulated (even maps are forbidden in an effort to prevent the inhabitants of each zone from locating the other zones). With the aid of an "access crystal" which the Sterlings acquire from a Zone Trooper not long after their arrival in Thel, each episode of *Otherworld* had the family fleeing through one of the various zones, pursued by the Zone Troopers and their leader, Commander Kroll (played by Jonathan Banks).

Starring Sam Groom and Gretchen Corbett as parents Hal and June Sterling, *Otherworld* suffered from an obvious lack of production values and budget, but made up for it with some trippy concepts and George Orwell/*1984*-esque ideologies, with the computer-based Church of Artificial Intelligence ruling over the zones with the power of absolute censorship and the right to condemn people to death for acts of perceived heresy. Marjoe Gortner guest starred in the fifth episode of the series, "Village of the Motorpigs." Directed by Paul Michael Glaser (best known for playing Starsky on *Starsky & Hutch*), the episode has the Sterling family being rescued from the Zone Troopers by a band of hippy-esque bikers, only to fall prey to their leader Chalktrauma (Marjoe), who keeps his followers in line with a potent hallucinogenic drug which they manufacture. Chalktrauma is also vehemently anti-family, splitting the Sterlings up to weaken their resistance and lessen the chance of them using their combined strength the challenge him and his position as leader of the Motorpigs.

Inspired perhaps by the off-beat George Romero film *Knightriders* (1981), "Village of the Motorpigs" climaxes with a medieval-style joust, with motorbikes substituting for horses (a concept that was earlier used for laughs in the classic 1967 episode of *Get Smart*, "The Mild Ones"). There's also a feel of the post-apocalyptic desert action genre popularized by *Mad Max 2* (aka *The Road Warrior*, 1982) about this episode, which helps make it quite enjoyable and one of the highpoints of the series. Dressed in leathers and fur, Marjoe looks to be having a good time and he once again plays a character not unlike an unbalanced religious cult leader, using spiritualism to explain his thirst for violence and to maintain control over his tribe ("I had a little talk to the Holy One and he said the unclean must be sacrificed").

Also appearing in "Village of the Motorpigs" are cult character actor Vincent Schiavelli and Jeff East, who played the young Clark Kent in Richard Donner's *Superman* (1978).

STREET HAWK
USA/ABC, 1985/13 episodes/60 minutes each
Creator: Paul M. Belous & Robert Wollerstorff
Regular cast: Rex Smith, Jeannie Wilson, Richard Venture & Joe Regalbuto
Episode: "The Adjuster", Season 1, Episode 3, 18 January, 1985

Inspired by the success of the popular *Knightrider* (1982–1986), *Street Hawk* was a fantasy action series with a comic book/superhero edge, starring Rex Smith as Jesse Mach, a Los Angeles motorcycle cop who is relegated to a desk job after being crippled in an assault. A shot at a new life and redemption comes to him when he is recruited by a top secret government agency to test ride the Street Hawk, a high-tech experimental motorbike designed to combat urban crime, equipped with tremendous firepower and capable of safely riding at speeds of up to 300 miles an hour. Receiving radical treatment to repair his legs in exchange for his participation in the program, Mach keeps up his facade of being a typical cop by day while donning black leathers and a helmet and fighting crime by night while patrolling the city on the Street Hawk. Only Norman Tuttle (Joe Regalbuto), the head of the Street Hawk program who monitors the bike's activities from a central control room, is aware of the true identity of the city's mysterious new protector.

Marjoe Gortner guest starred in the third episode of *Street Hawk*, "The Adjuster." Directed by Virgil W. Vogel (who also directed Marjoe in his *Airwolf* appearance), "The Adjuster" pits Jesse Mach against tough New York cop Joseph Cannon (Marjoe), who has been sent to L.A. to extradite an embezzler that has been captured by the Street Hawk. When Cannon goes berserk after the embezzler escapes his custody at LAX, Mach suspects there is more to the story than meets the eye, and with the help of Tuttle he soon discovers that the real Joseph Cannon has been found murdered in New York, and the man sent to L.A. in his place is an enforcer trying to recover half a million in cash which the embezzler had stolen from a big New York crime figure. The mysterious villain (whose real name is never revealed) eventually tracks down the embezzler at an abandoned merry-go-round at Venice Beach, plugging him full of holes and making off with the stolen loot for himself, with the Street Hawk in hot pursuit, before being killed in an old condemned theatre that is being dynamited by a demolition crew.

Marjoe really chews his way through some scenery in "The Adjuster", making a particularly memorable entrance as he barges his way through the L.A. police station, elbowing a cop to the ground and telling the police commander that it's "hard to tell who's who around here, the whole place reeks of hair spray." Though it only lasted thirteen episodes, *Street Hawk* was hyped enough to inspire a small rash of spin-off merchandise, including a Kenner toy motorcycle, model kits, walkie talkies, paperback novels and a Colorforms adventure set. It's somewhat surprising that the series did not find a larger audience and last longer, as it is quite an entertaining show, and lead Rex Smith was something of a teen idol at the time, having scored a Top 10 hit single with "You Take My Breath Away" in 1979 and playing the lead role of Fredric in *The Pirates of Penzance* on stage as well as in the 1980 TV movie and 1983 feature film adaptation. *Street Hawk* also benefited from having its theme music composed and performed by the German avante garde group Tangerine Dream.

THE GREAT RIDE
USA/FOX SPORTS, 2011/5 episodes/60 minutes each
Writer & Director: Jeff Androsky

After virtually disappearing from his life in front of the cameras in the mid–nineties, Marjoe Gortner made a rare television appearance in this short–lived sports and lifestyle series which aired on the Fox Sports network and celebrated the freedom and excitement of exploring America on two wheels. Hosted by Brian Corsetti and directed by Jeff Androsky, Marjoe appeared as himself in all five episodes of *The Great Ride*, sharing tube time with other celebrities and fringe personalities like Peter Fonda, Robert Davi and Evel Knievel's son Robbie (a stunt motorcyclist like his father).

CHAPTER FIVE

Marjoe on Wax: Soundtracks & Recordings

MARJOE'S FIRST FORAY into recording was via a triple ten–inch record set of his child sermons, which was titled *World's Youngest Evangelist* and privately pressed and sold through the pages of the *Twilight Tidings* newsletter as well at his revival meetings, both during Marjoe's childhood and when he later returned to Pentecostal preaching in his late–twenties.

The first Marjoe albums were recorded at Sacred Records, a Los Angeles–based studio that was established by youth minister Earle E. Williams in 1944 and specialized in releasing religious–themed music. Later recordings were captured live on the road during Marjoe's sermons and included such incendiary tracks as "Hell with the Lid Off." Copies of Marjoe's albums (which can be briefly glimpsed being hawked to audiences in the *Marjoe* documentary) are now very scarce and rarely turn up for sale. However, some of the tracks were later reused on the soundtrack LP to *Marjoe*, which was released in 1972 on the Warner Brothers label. Featuring a fiery red, orange and yellow cover, with a distorted B&W photo of a sweaty Marjoe caught in mid–rapture, the *Marjoe* soundtrack makes a perfect souvenir and aural companion piece to the documentary. Along with the early recordings, the soundtrack also features some of the adult Marjoe's sermons as heard in the film, and concludes with *"Save all my Brothers (Love Theme from Marjoe")*, a track co–written by Sarah Kernochan and Joseph Brooks and performed by Jerry Keller (an Arkansas singer/songwriter who had a hit with *"Here Comes Summer"* in 1958 and had composed, with Van Alexander, the soundtrack to William Castle's enjoyable 1965 thriller *I Saw What You Did*).

Original 8 track release of Marjoe's *Bad But Not Evil* album, issued by Chelsea Records in 1972.

Riding high on the critical success and notoriety of *Marjoe*, 1972 also saw Gortner release his one and only full-length musical LP, which was titled *Bad But Not Evil* (after a line he used in the documentary) and issued on the Chelsea label in America and by RCA Victor in the UK. Produced by the prolific songwriter/producer Wes Farrell (who found huge success as the producer and co-writer for The Partridge Family and had founded Chelsea Records earlier that year), *Bad But Not Evil* contained nine tracks, mostly consisting of covers and performed in a folk, blues and gospel style, with a touch of pop-rock to try and give it a bit of radio and commercial potential. The album kicks off on a rousing note with the catchy and somewhat ambiguously titled "Hoe Bus", but the most prominent track on the album was Bob Dylan's "Lo and Behold!", which was released as a single and managed to reach #109 on the *Billboard* singles chart (the October 28, 1972 edition of *Billboard* featured "Lo and Behold!" in their Radio Action and Pick Singles section, with reviewer Don Ovens observing: *"The hot property now burning up the movie screens around the country makes a strong disc debut with equally strong Bob Dylan rhythm ballad material."*) A follow-up single, "Collection Box" b/w "I'm the Man" was released in the US and some overseas territories like France, but saw negligible chart action or air play. A promotional 7" of "Glory Hallelujah" b/w "I Shall Be Released" (another Dylan composition) was also issued in France.

One of the female backing vocalists on *Bad But Not Evil* was New Yorker Venetta Fields, who had worked with the likes of Ike and Tina Turner, Pink Floyd and the Rolling Stones, before she moved to Australia in 1982 and found continued success both on stage and as a backing singer for popular Australian rock acts such as Cold Chisel, Jimmy Barnes, Australian Crawl and John Farnham.

After *Bad But Not Evil* came and went without a whole lot of fanfare or sales, Marjoe wisely concentrated on his burgeoning film and television career, though he did briefly relive his pop star ambitions by playing murderous rocker David Colton on *Barnaby Jones* and belting out of some classic rock & roll numbers as part of his guest starring role in the "Return of the Big Rocker" episode of *Whiz Kids* (as well as performing the opening two lines of *"Jailhouse Rock"* while breaking out of a Mexican jail in *Acapulco Gold*).

Spanish picture sleeve for the 7" single release of *Hoe Bus b/w Low and Behold!*, issued on the RCA Victor label.

CHAPTER SIX

Marjoe: The Enduring Enigma

SINCE HIS VIRTUAL disappearance from the cameras and public life in the late–1990s, the question has often been asked: whatever happened to Marjoe Gortner, and what is he doing today? When I set out to write this book, I of course made many attempts to track the man down, not just in the hopes of getting his input, but just to make him aware of the project and getting his blessings for it. Unfortunately, all roads led to an ultimate dead end. I kept pushing back the completion deadline for the book in the hope that I would have a breakthrough, but it seemed like I was not the only one frustrated by Marjoe's present whereabouts. Most of the people I interviewed for the book were just as lost as to where he might be, and had not been in contact with him for many years. Some promising leads did occasionally turn up, but always ended in disappointment. Emails and phone calls to a high–end New York lawyer that had supposedly represented Marjoe in the past went unanswered. I managed to track down his daughter Gigi but she merely dismissed my book as "fake news', despite the fact that it had not even been completed yet, and despite reassurances from myself that *Wildcat!* was not going to be salacious bio looking for dirt but a genuine appreciation of her father's work from a lifelong admirer. I also got in contact with his nephew, Brian Gortner, who was friendly and supportive of the project but unfortunately had not had contact with either his uncle of his own father for many years (Brian's strong atheism seemed to be the primary reason behind the lost communication). Brian was, however, nice enough to send me some great photos of the array of rare old Marjoe memorabilia which he had inherited (all of it pertaining to his child evangelist days).

Some of the interviewees for *Wildcat!* provided wildly varying theories behind Marjoe's apparent retreat from the public eye. One even suggested he was in hiding from vengeful Pentecostal ministers who wanted him dead out of a lingering grudge over his *Marjoe* documentary! Sarah Kernochan, the co–director of *Marjoe*, told me the last time she had had any contact with Gortner was in the early–2000s, when the film was finally getting its long–awaited DVD release. In her words, Marjoe did not seem at all enthused or impressed that the documentary was about to resurface.

One person who had a rare encounter with Marjoe in the late–nineties was filmmaker Jeff Lieberman, the writer/director of memorable cult hits like *Squirm* (1976), *Blue Sunshine* (1977) and *Remote Control* (1988), who related this little anecdote to me:

"When I went to a New York City midtown hotel to pick up my Rolling Stones VIP tickets he was right there doing the same. Nobody but me recognized him (or even knew anything about him for that matter) but I sure did and we had a great chat. Organized religion has always been synonymous with show business and his story exemplifies that perfectly."

Most people I spoke to agreed that Marjoe would prove a very popular attraction at the celebrity autograph conventions that attract so many collectors today, where actors, musicians, directors and other pop culture personalities, usually from the 1960s–90s, meet fans and sign photographs, memorabilia and pose for selfies (all for a fee, of course). Conventions can be an extremely lucrative way for semi or fully-retired actors in their later years to make some decent spending money, keep themselves in the public eye, and shoot the breeze about the good old days. But maybe Marjoe needs neither the dollars nor the adulation (nor neither the humiliation?). But there is also the possibility that a more cynical or bleak reason may be behind Marjoe's distancing himself from the public eye over the past two decades. Maybe he found his film and television career to be ultimately not what he had planned or hoped for it to be, and has grown bitter from the disappointment and chose to just completely shut himself off from it. Maybe it really was all just a means to an end and the easiest method for Marjoe to use his past as a way to replenish the significant fortune in cash that he had earned for his parents decades earlier, but never got to enjoy a cent of? If Gortner had no true love or passion for the art and craft of acting, it would hardly be an environment he would want to continue hovering around once he had effectively given up (though paparazzi photos of the time indicate that he certainly enjoyed his celebrity status). It's also just as possible that the roles simply started to dry up, and Marjoe decided to bow out gracefully, but at this point much of it is sadly speculation.

Rather than let myself become frustrated, I decided instead to accept and embrace the mystique. In many ways, it made perfect sense. Though he lived so much of it in the public eye, Marjoe's life remains as much of an enigma today as always. At this point it can only be speculative as to how he looks back upon his acting career, and how fulfilling he found it. While some may argue the creative merits of the work he often appeared in, he should be applauded and admired for making it all work in his favor. Not many people get the chance for a public reinvention, and even fewer manage to pull it off as successfully.

A rare recent public appearance for Marjoe came on September 28, 2018, when he was photographed attending a "Hollywood Royalty Dinner" at the famous Hearst Castle in San Simeon, California. Sporting long-ish hair, now white and slicked straight back, and wearing lightly-tinted glasses and a black suit offset by a frilly white shirt and an enormous flared tie bearing a bold Native American/Aztec pattern, Marjoe certainly looks distinctive amongst the other male guests. But I found the magnificent grandness of the location to be a perfect environment for the Marjoe Gortner of today to be found in. Built between 1919 and 1947 by newspaper magnate William Randolph Hearst in collaboration with architect Julia Morgan, and situated on 40,000 acres of land by the California coast, the opulence of Hearst Castle seems akin to the same sort of opulence and over-indulgence in which today's more successful televangelists shamelessly wallow in.

Marjoe turned 75-years-old on January 14, 2019. While there is always the chance of him performing another public career reappearance—or perhaps resurrection is a better word—the likelihood seems slimmer and slimmer as time marches on.

When you comin' back, Marjoe Gortner?

APPENDIX 1:
Bibliography

(Note: Books and magazines are listed alphabetically).

Books:

Are You in the House Alone? Edited by Amanda Reyes

(Headpress/338 pages/2016/UK)

A compendium book which looks at American TV movies produced between 1964–1999. Includes a review of *Pray for the Wildcats*.

Cult Movie Stars by Danny Peary

(Fireside/608 pages/1991/USA)

An A–Z listing of actors who have established cult followings of varying size and devotion. Includes an entry on Marjoe Gortner, accompanied by a B&W still of him with Candy Clark in *When You Comin' Back, Red Ryder*.

Cults in America by David Hanna

(Belmont Tower/284 pages/1979/USA)

Mass market paperback no doubt rushed out to capitalize on the publicity following the tragic mass–suicide committed in Guyana by over 900 members of Peoples' Temple, the religious cult led by Jim Jones, who had taken his followers to South America after authorities in San Francisco started investigating the church's activities. *Cults in America* features sections on Jones as well as other notorious cult leaders such as Charles Manson, modern followers of the Marquis de Sade, the American Nazi Party and others. Chapter Four of the paperback ("Passport to Shangri–La") features a five–page piece on Marjoe Gortner sub-titled "Evangelical Superstar at Four", which provides a brief encapsulation of Marjoe's public childhood and adult comeback. David Hanna was a prolific author of paperback bios, penning titles on John Wayne, Humphrey Bogart, Frank Sinatra, Elvis Presley, *Valley of the Dolls* author Jaqueline Susann and several notorious crime and mob figures including Bugsy Siegel, Carlo Gambino and Vito Genovese.

Earthquake by George Fox

(Signet/128 pages/1974/USA)

Paperback tie–in for the *Earthquake* film, written by the film's co–screenwriter. The first half of the book is a straight novelization of the film's story, while the second half documents the making of the movie. Includes photos of Marjoe on the back cover and the film's black & white photo section, as well as a brief paragraph about the casting of Marjoe in the making of section).

Evel Incarnate by Steve Mandich

(Sidgwick & Jackson/256 pages/2000/UK)

Biography of Evel Knievel. Includes four pages on the making of *Viva Knievel!* with Marjoe. B&W photo of Marjoe with Knievel from the film included amongst the book's photo pages.

Paperback edition of Steven Gaines' essential Marjoe bio, published in 1974 by Dell.

Marjoe by Steven Gaines

(Harper & Row/238 pages/1973/USA)

Original hardcover publication of the classic Marjoe biography. Illustrated with black & white photo sections.

Marjoe by Steven Gaines

(Dell/236 pages/1974/USA)

Mass market paperback reprinting of the Gaines biography. Same text but no photographs and a cover design that—in keeping with the traditions of the lurid paperback market at the time—is somewhat more garish and exploitive than the hardcover (*"Turn on to the Holy Hustler! The book that goes even further than the movie!"*, screams the cover blurb).

Massacred by Mother Nature by Lee Gambin

(Midnight Marquee Press/220 pages/2012/USA)

An examination of the 'nature amok' sub-genre of horror cinema, popularized in the seventies by movies like *Jaws* (1974), *Grizzly* (1976) and *Piranha*. Written by Australian film historian and passionate fan Lee Gambin, *Massacred by Mother Nature* devotes several pages to covering *The Food of the Gods* and has some nice things to say about Marjoe's performance in the film ("Former child preacher Marjoe Gortner just shines as the heroic protagonist with his wiry frame, thick locks of curly hair and snappy delivery of some wonderful one-liners").

The Psychotronic Encyclopedia of Film by Michael J. Weldon

(Ballantine Books/672 pages/1983/USA)

A seminal and very influential cinema book, *The Psychotronic Encyclopedia of Film* arrived at the perfect time to provide the exploitation fan with an educational roadmap through all the old genre films and drive–in B–movies which were starting to find a new life, along with a new audience, on the home video market which was just starting to really explode at that point. Author Michael J. Weldon had previously self–published the hand–written *Psychotronic* weekly newsletter, which reviewed all the horror, exploitation and other genre films which were being screened on television in New York that week. He would later publish 41 issues of the classic *Psychotronic Video* magazine between 1989–2006. *The Psychotronic Encyclopedia of Film* includes capsule reviews of the Marjoe movies *Earthquake*, *Food of the Gods* and *Starcrash*.

The Psychotronic Video Guide by Michael J. Weldon

(St. Martin's Griffin/646 pages/1996/USA)

Weldon's follow–up to *The Psychotronic Encyclopedia of Film* expands the scope of the first book to cover genres like 80s action, direct–to–video 90s erotic thrillers, and more. Another essential book for lovers of exploitation and low–brow cinema, *The Psychotronic Video Guide* includes entries on a number of Marjoe Gortner movies, including *American Ninja 3: Blood Sport*, *Marjoe*, *Hellhole* and *Viva Knievel!*

Magazines:

Below is a listing of recommended magazines featuring interviews or articles about Marjoe Gortner and/or his movies.

After Dark Volume 5, No. 6, October 1972 (USA)

(Two–page illustrated article on Marjoe entitled "Marjoe Gortner: Twice on Sundays" by Norma McLain Stoop).

Famous Monsters of Filmland No. 128, September 1978 (USA)

(Eight–page illustrated article on *The Food of the Gods*, featuring several photos of Marjoe from the movie).

Famous Monsters of Filmland No. 181, March 1982 (USA)

(Three–page illustrated article on *Mausoleum* focusing mostly on female star Bobbie Bresee, no photos or mention of Marjoe).

Fangoria No. 28, July 1983 (USA)

(Four–page illustrated interview with John Buechler, the makeup artist who worked on *Mausoleum*. Includes a color set photo of Buechler applying the gory, gaping wound to Marjoe's chest).

High Society's Celebrity Skin Special Collector's Edition 1984 (Australia)

(Seven–page illustrated article on Lynda Carter and her nude scenes in *Bobbie Jo and the Outlaw*. Includes several color photos and frame blow–ups of Carter with Marjoe).

Is it….Uncut? Special No. 2, 2003 (UK)

(UK publication devoted to horror, cult and exploitation cinema. Includes review of *When You Comin' Back, Red Ryder* by John Harrison).

19 Magazine June 1979 (UK)

(UK lifestyle magazine aimed at females in their mid–to–upper-teens. Contains a two–page feature titled "Marjoe Gortner—From Pulpit to Silver Screen).

Oui May 1974 (USA)

(A men's magazine from the publishers of *Playboy*. Features an article written by Marjoe Gortner covering the appearance of fifteen–year–old guru Maharaj Ji at the Millennium '73 peace convention held at the Huston Astrodome).

Bibliography

People Weekly June 26 1978 (USA)

(Three-page illustrated article on Marjoe, written by Lois Armstrong for the magazine's regular "Couples" feature. Covers Marjoe's Mexican marriage to Candy Clark and the making of *When You Comin Back, Red Ryder*).

Penthouse Volume 4, Number 6, February 1973 (USA)

(Six-page interview with Marjoe by Francis Feighan).

Psychotronic Video No. 34, 2001 (USA)

(Interview with Jesse Vint, who talks briefly about working with Marjoe in *Earthquake* and *Bobbie Jo and the Outlaw*).

Shock Cinema No. 18, Spring-Summer 2001 (USA)

(Review of *When You Comin' Back, Red Ryder* by Steve Puchalski).

Swank Vol. 27, No. 12, December 1980 (USA)

(A long-running men's magazine which first appeared in 1941 and was originally published by Fox Comics. Features an interview with Marjoe by Fred Robbins, conducted around the time that Gortner was co-hosting *Speak Up, America*).

TV Times October 11–17 1980 (USA)

(Weekly television magazine featuring cover story on Marjoe and Jayne Kennedy promoting *Speak Up, America*).

AVAILABILITY

The following Marjoe Gortner feature films, telemovies and episodic TV shows have all been officially released on Blu-ray and/or DVD (label listed in brackets indicates the most recent release as of this book's publication). Titles listed alphabetically. All are US releases unless otherwise noted. Check eBay, Amazon and other online retail sources for availability.

Feature Films/Telemovies:

Acapulco Gold (Blu-ray, Code Red)

American Ninja 3: Blood Hunt (DVD, Olive Films)

Bobbie Jo and the Outlaw (Blu-ray, Kino Lorber)

Earthquake (Blu-ray, Universal)

Fire, Ice & Dynamite (DVD, Payless)

Food of the Gods (Blu-ray, released by Shout! Factory as a double-bill with 1972's *Frogs*)

The Gun and the Pulpit (Miracle Pictures, also released on several other budget labels, both individually and in double packs and even as part of a ten-movie western box set).

Jungle Warriors (Panik House Entertainment, released in a three-film set with two Linda Blair women-in-prison titles, the notorious *Chained Heat* [1983] and *Red Heat* [1985]).

Hellhole (Blu-ray, Shout! Factory)

The Marcus-Nelson Murders (DVD, Umbrella Entertainment, Australia)

Mausoleum (Blu-ray, Vinegar Syndrome)

Marjoe (DVD, Docurama)

Mayday at 40,000 Feet (DVD, Warner Archive)

Pray for the Wildcats (DVD, Echo Bridge)

Starcrash (Blu-ray, Shout! Factory)

Viva Knievel (DVD, Warner)

When You Comin' Back, Red Ryder (DVD, Umbrella Entertainment, Australia)

Wild Bill (Blu-ray, Twilight Time)

Note: *Sidewinder 1* has also been offered as a bootleg DVD, of varying quality, by several public domain sellers. The best version seems to be the one offered by the Just For the Hell of It label (www.j4hi.com), who have it available as a two–disc set, paired with another rare dirt bike adventure film, 1979's *A Great Ride*).

Television Shows:

Airwolf (DVD, Mill Creek Entertainment)

The A-Team (DVD, Universal)

Barnaby Jones (DVD, Visual Entertainment)

Falcon Crest (DVD, Warner Brothers)

Fantasy Island (DVD, Sony Pictures)

Hotel (DVD, Visual Entertainment)

Matt Houston (DVD, Visual Entertainment)

Police Story (DVD, Shout! Factory)

Street Hawk (DVD, Shout! Factory)

T. J. Hooker (DVD, Shout! Factory)

Whiz Kids (DVD, Elephant Films, France)

Note: *Whiz Kids*, currently only available as a legitimate release from France (on a rather poor quality four–disc set that is missing five episodes but includes "Return of the Big Rocker"). It is also available from various bootleg and grey–market DVD sources.

American VHS release of *Marjoe*, along with the Argentinian VHS of *When You Comin' Back, Red Ryder*, retitled *Perversión* for that market.

Afterword
By Lee Gambin

A PERSONAL TIP of the hat to both Marjoe Gortner and John Harrison…

I love that historian and author John Harrison has written this loving tribute to the legend that is Marjoe Gortner for a number of reasons—but the primary one has to be the fact that Marjoe is someone that I too have always been fascinated by. I mean, what an enigma of entertainment—and when I use that term, I mean both on the film star front as well as being a child preacher! Upon watching the documentary *Marjoe* (1972) I became even more invested in learning about this charismatic curly-haired former revival-tent Evangelist who turned movie star, and John's book is a perfect examination and exploration into Gortner's work.

I first became aware of Marjoe as a kid when I first saw *Food of the Gods* (1976), a movie I quickly became obsessed with him—from the incredible sequence where Marjoe fights off a giant rooster, to the excellent cast headed by the likes of icon and pioneer Ida Lupino, to that marvelous one sheet poster art where the giant rat is leering over the hapless victim sprawled over a tree branch, and mostly for those wonderful moments throughout the film—that are relentless—where mammoth rodents terrorize Marjoe and co. I mean this was just horror movie bliss for a kid addicted to monsters and gore.

Years later, as an adult and when working on my book on eco-horror films, I interviewed director Bert I. Gordon, the B-movie giant (and Mr. B.I.G. to us monster movie fans) and that is something that people like John and I are endlessly doing—not only critically discussing movies, but also reaching out and talking with people who were involved! To go from being a kid sitting in front of the TV screen eternally watching movies of all kinds over and over again to someone now working in the field as a film historian/writer, is a major coup and to hear stories about people like Marjoe (who remain so mysterious) was always awesome. Of course, when talking to Bert, the conversation was primarily about his entries in the natural horror subgenre; therefore, we talked about the grasshopper sci-fi classic *Beginning of the End* (1957), the Joan Collins monster movie triumph *Empire of the Ants* (1977) and of course, the aforementioned *Food of the Gods* (which would be my favorite out of the three). Bert mostly talked about Joan Collins and her battling giant ants (but mostly fighting harsh conditions where they shot) and the endless struggles he had with grasshoppers for his fifties entry, and therefore conversations about Marjoe went undiscussed, which was slightly disappointing, but nevertheless possibly understandable.

So, for that reason alone, it is super important that John's book exists! When asked to write the liner notes for Arrow Video's release of *Children of the Corn* (1984), I decided against going the obvious route (no talk on Stephen King or the film itself really) and wrote instead about child preachers who I have always been fascinated by—in fact, preachers in the tent-revival scenario in general have always interested me as a bizarre, sideshow, circus-style oddity. Films about crazed preachers always appealed—*Elmer Gantry* (1960), *Angel Baby* (1961) et al, and then when I started researching the likes of Uldine Utley, Solomon Burke and Marjoe, this wave of child preachers was both bizarrely intriguing and also terrifying—something likened to what I mentioned earlier, the role of the sideshow performer.

So this combo of having a history of being this pint-sized cherubic crazed fore-warner of fire and damnation and growing into a cult movie legend who delivered some meaty, brilliant performances (most notably as the terrifying Vietnam vet holding people captive in a Texan diner in *When You Comin' Back Red Ryder?* [1979]) makes for a worthy idol to be worshipped and honored – or at the very least, not forgotten.

Lee Gambin

(Lee Gambin is a Bram Stoker and Rondo-nominated film historian and writer whose books include *Massacred by Mother Nature: Exploring the Natural Horror Film*, *The Howling: Studies in the Horror Film*, *We Can Be Who We Are: Movie Musicals from the 1970s*, *Hell Hath No Fury Like Her: The Making of Christine* and *Nope, Nothing Wrong Here: The Making of Cujo*, the last three titles published by Bear Manor).

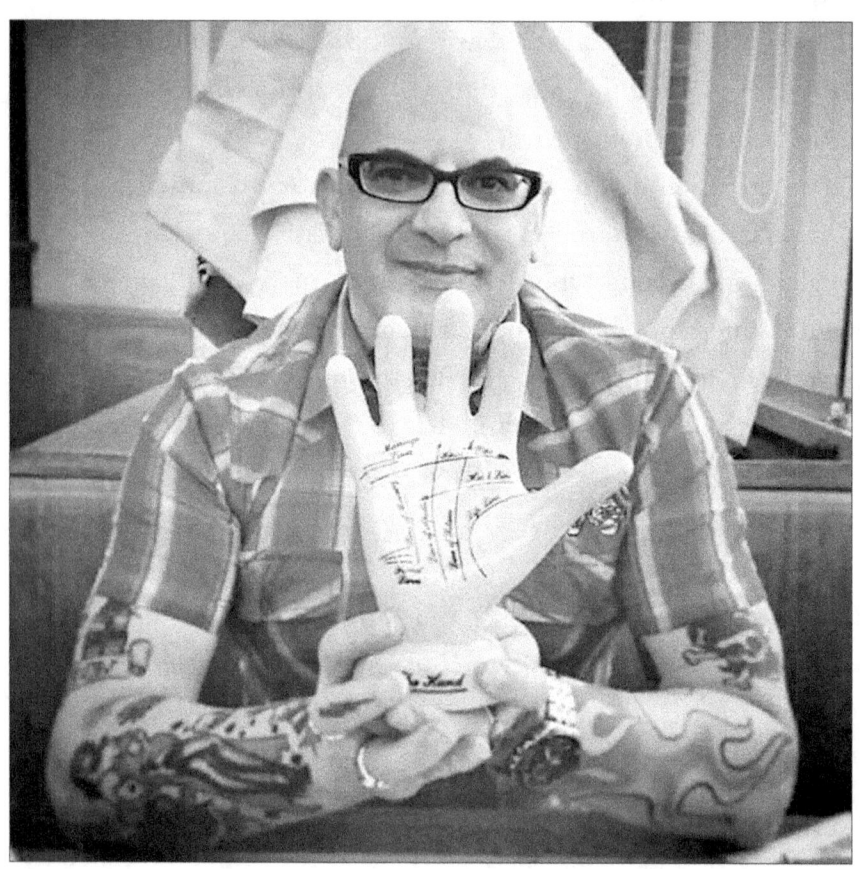

Author John Harrison.

About the Author

JOHN HARRISON IS a freelance writer and film historian based in Melbourne, Australia. His previous books include *Hip Pocket Sleaze: The Lurid World of Vintage Adult Paperbacks*, *Blood on the Windscreen: The Cold and Violent World of the Driver's Education Film 1959–1975* and *Reel Wild Cinema!*, the later a compendium of his 1990s fanzine devoted to eclectic film and video.

In addition to writing for publications such as *Monster!*, *Weng's Chop* and *The Cinemaniacs Journal*, Harrison has also contributed reviews and liner notes for many DVD and VHS releases from the ground-breaking Something Weird Video company, and penned the booklet essays for the Australian Blu-ray releases of *Thirst* (1979), *The Survivor* (1981) and *Dead Kids* (1982).

As a six-time nominee at the Rondo Hatton Classic Horror Awards, Harrison has also recorded Blu-ray audio commentaries and introduced screenings of cult films presented by the Cinemaniacs Film Collective in Melbourne. In 2014, he introduced a screening of *When You Comin; Back, Red Ryder?* at a film fair in Northcote. An avid collector of vintage pop culture esoterica (including true crime and monster movie magazines, pulp paperbacks, horror comics, 8mm adult film reels and Las Vegas memorabilia from the 1950s–1980s), his upcoming works include a biography of actress/singer/composer/former Hollywood stuntwoman Marneen Lynne

Fields, whom he married at the Little White Wedding Chapel in Las Vegas on March 20, 2016.

    Blog: www.john-harrison.blogspot.com

    Email: jharrison666@yahoo.com.au

Thank You

Amongst those I would like to extend a grateful and heartfelt thanks are: Belinda Balaski, Luigo Cozzi, Betsey Crockett–Lassiter, Lee Gambin, Brian Gortner, Pete Howlett, Andrew Leavold, Sarah Kernochan and Cedric Sundstrom. Apologies to anyone I may have inadvertently missed. And of course, extra special thanks to my beautiful wife Marneen for both her encouragement, inspiration and patience during the writing of this book.

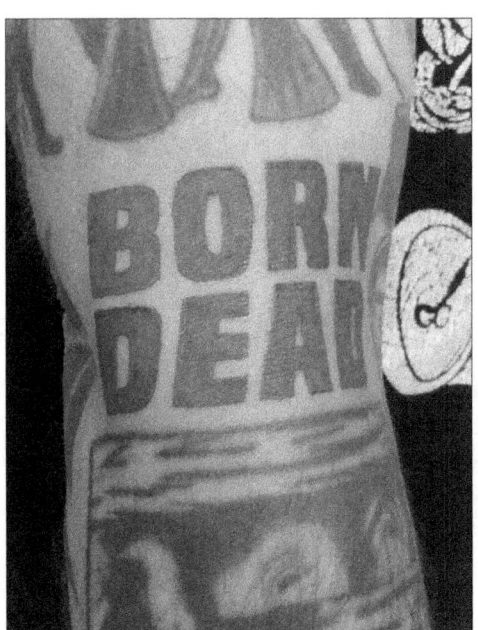

"Born Dead." A 2019 tattoo inked on noted South Australian punk musician (and ardent Marjoe Gortner fan) Pete Howlett, designed in tribute to *When You Comin' Back, Red Ryder*.

Index

Numbers in **bold** indicate photographs

A–Team, The 193-194, 223
ABC's Wide World of Entertainment 168-169
Acapulco Gold 80-85, **83**, 210, 222
Ackerman, Forrest J. 86, 131
"Adjuster, The" 204-205
Airport 53-54, 55, 92, 194
Airwolf 198-201, 204, 223
Allen, Irwin 54-55, 95, 100, 156, 175
Allen, Sheila 100
American Ninja 3: Blood Hunt 151-158, **154**, 219, 222
Arcangeli, Marina 135-136
Archer 180
Archerd, Army **168**
Arkoff, Lou 122, 136, 139, 144, 145-146
Arkoff, Sam 85, 122, 123

"Baby Come Back" 71
Bad But Not Evil 32, 177-178, **208**, 209-210
Balaski, Belinda 62, 64, 68-80, **70**, 85, 87
Bare, Bobby 72
Barnaby Jones 175-178, 210, 223

Bellamy, Earl 103, 105-106
Black Eye 68-69
Bobbie Jo and the Outlaw 62-67, **63**, 68-77, **70**, 220, 221, 222
Bogner, Willy 158, 160
Bradley, David 151, 153
Brand, Neville 172, 174
Brenner, Jules 113-114
Bresee, Bobbie 124, 126, **130**, 130-131, 220
Bridges, Jeff 162, 163, 165
Brinckerhoff, Burt 80, 84-85
Broadway on Showtime 183-184
Brooks, Joseph 208
Brother Lucas 17
Brown, Alma 5
Buechler, John Carl 127, 220
Bundy, Brooke 175
Burns, Robert A. 129
Butler, Robert 92, 95

Camillo, Tony 150
Carter, Lynda 62, **63**, 63, 67, 69, **70**, 71, 72, 73, 75, 76-77, 220
Casaro, Renato 161, **162**
Chakiras, George 156
Chan, Michele 151, 154, **154**, 155
Chesnut, Jerry 169
Circus of the Stars 159, 185-186

231

Clark, Candy xiii, 106, 107, **107**, 113, 116, 215, 221
Clinton, George S. 155
Coates, Lewis see Cozzi, Luigi
"Cobra Strikes, The" 155
"Collection Box" 209
Conway, Gary 151, 155-156
Corey, Jeff 47, 51
Corman, Roger 117, 131, 139
Courtney, Chuck 87, **88**
Cozzi, Luigi 117-118, 120, 121-124, **122**, 145
Crawford, Broderick **93**, 93
Crowley, J. C. 71-72
Cunningham, Herbert 11

Dalzell, Dennis 104
Dam Busters, The 201
"Dambreakers" 198-201
Danning, Sybil 131, 135, 137
Davis, Gary Charles 102
De Moro, Pierre 136, **141**, 146
DeGuere, Philip 195, 196-197, 198
"Demi-God" 167
Dickinson, Angie 41, 45
Douglas, Gordon 96, 102-103
Dressler, Lieux 69
Dryer, Robert 190, 191
Dudikoff, Michael 152-153, 156
Dylan, Bob 209

Earthquake 31, 52-62, **59**, **61**, 79, 149, 216, 219, 221, 222
Ebert, Roger 33
Ebsen, Buddy 175-176
Evel Knievel (1971) 97-98
Evel Knievel on Tour 102
Evers, Jason 178

Falcon Crest 34, 187-189, 223
Fantasy Island 34, 84, 184-185, 195, 223
Faracy, Stephanie 106, 113
Farrell, Wes 209
Fields, Marneen 136, 139, 140-146, **141**, **145**, **146**
Fields, Venetta 209
Fire, Ice & Dynamite 158-162, **162**, 222
Firth, Peter 106, 113
Food of the Gods, The xii, 68, 73, 76, 77-80, **85**, 85-91, **88**, **91**, 122, 123, 218, 220, 222, 225, 226
"Four in the Morning" 169

Gaines, Steven xii, xv, **217**, 218
Gambin, Lee 218, 225-227
Gardner, Ava 52, 56
Gary, Lorraine 35, 40, 41, 42, 45
Ginty, Robert 174-175
Glaser, Paul Michael 203
"Glory Hallelujah" 209
"Gold Record for Murder, A" 175-178
Gordon, Bert I. xii, 77-78, 84, 85, 86-87, 89, 90, 226
Gortner, Agnes Benjamin 25
Gortner, Ann 11, 12-13, 15
Gortner, Brian 212
Gortner, Gigi 11, 211
Gortner, Marge 2, 3, 4, 5, 6, 8, 10, 11, 20, 68, 72, 75
Gortner, Narver 1
Gortner, Ross 1
Gortner, Starloe 10, 11
Gortner, Vernoe 3, 8, 10
Gortner, Vernon 1-3, 4, 6, 8, 10-11, 15-16, 25

Index

Grant, Lee 106, **112**, 113
"Great Balls of Fire" 197
Great Ride, The 206
Greene, Lorne 52, 56
Griffith, Andy 41-42, **42**, 45
Gun and the Pulpit, The 47-52, 222

Hamilton, George 97, 98
Hamilton, Murray 172, 174
Harpaz, Udi 201
Harrison, George 14
Heart Outright, The 116-117
"Hell with the Lid Off" 207
Hellhole 136-146, **138**, **141**, **146**, 219, 222
Helter Skelter 114, 150
Henneberger, Barbara 160
Heston, Charlton 52, 56
Hill, Walter 162, 163
Hingle, Pat 106, 113
"Hoe Bus" 209, **210**
Hollander, Stephanie 13-17, 25
Hopper, Dennis 133-134
Hotel 194-195, 223
Howard, Susan 103, 104, 105
Husky, Rick 189, 190
Hutton, Lauren 96, 98, 101

"I Shall Be Released" 209
"I'm the Man" 209
"Images" 194-195

Jack Tillman: The Survivalist see Survivalist, The
"Jailhouse Rock" 210
James, Steve 151, 152-153, 154
Jungle Warriors 131-136, **134**, 222

Katselas, Milton 106, 111, **115**
Kauppi, Lisa 155
Keller, Jerry 208
Kelly, Gene 96, 98, **100**
Kennedy, Jayne 186, 221
Kernochan, Sarah 19, 25-26, 27, 28-32, 208, 212
Klein, Steve 13
Knievel, Evel 96-103, **100**, 206, 216
Kojak 35-41

Ladd, Margaret 188, 189
"Lag Time" 189, 191-192
Lancaster, Burt 53, 54
Landers, Judy 136, 137, 139
Lansing, Robert 80, 81, 84
Laugh-In 181-182
Laverne, Flo 2-3, 7
Leap of Faith 27
Lester, Mark L. 62-63, 66, 69, 71-72, 74, 75, 77
Lewis, Geoffrey 47, 49, 51
Lewis, Robert Michael 41
License to Kill 159
Lieberman, Jeff 90, 212
Linden, Hal 106, **112**, 113
Lindley, Audra 106, 113
"Lo and Behold!" 209, **210**
Lo Bianco, Tony 170, 171
"Loving Strangers/Something Borrowed, Something Blue…" 184-185, 195
Lupino, Ida 77-78, 85, 87, 225

Mann, Abby 35-36
Marcus–Nelson Murders, The 31, 35-41, **38**, 171, 222

Marjoe 19-32, **21**, **28**, 33, 56, 69, 72, 75, 76, 207-208, 209, 212, 225
Marjoe: A Modern Miracle 7
"Marjoe's Country: Nashville" 168-169,
Martin, Pamela Sue 47, 48, 51, 55
Matt Houston 192, 223
Mattson, Robin 179-180
Mausoleum 34, 124-131, **126**, **130**, 220, 222
Mayday at 40,000 Feet! 92-95, **93**, 223
McCowan, George 178
McKinney, Bill 106, 113
McMillan, Marge see Gortner, Marge
Medical Center 167
Medoff, Mark 106, 110, 113, 116, 117
Meeker, Ralph 78, 85, 88
Milius, John 98
Milland, Ray 92
Miller, Raymond 5-6
Moore, Roger 158, 160, **162**, 182
"Moving Target, The" 179-180
Mr. T 193
Munro, Caroline 117, 118, 120, 121, **122**
Myrow, Fred 45

Nakia 179-180
Neame, Ronald 55
Nelson, Ed 80, 84
Nelson, Gary 180
Newton, Wayne 159
Nielsen, Leslie 96, **100**, 101, 186
Nitzsche, Jack 114
Norris, Chuck 116, 152

Oakes, Randi 80, 82, **83**, 84
"Old Time Rock and Roll" 197
Otherworld 201-203
Ovens, Don 209

Palmer, Gene 60
Parks, Michael 103, 105, **105**, 172
Pearce, Richard 27
Pembroke, Don 156-157
Pescow, Donna 195
Petrie, Daniel 47, 50
Pickens, Slim 47, 48, 51
Police Story 34, 169-175, 223
Poseidon Adventure, The 51, 55-56
Potter, Forrest 9
Pray for the Wildcats 31, 40, 41-47, **42**, 215, 223
Principal, Victoria 52, 56, 57, **59**, 60, **61**, 62
Puzo, Mario 52, 58

Rae, Charlotte 103, 104
Railsback, Steve 147, 148, 149-150
Rains, Chick 72
"Recipe for Heavy Bread" 193-194
Reed, Robert 41, 42, **42**
"Requiem for an Informer" 169, 170-171
"Return of the Big Rocker" 195-198, 210, 224
"Revenge of the Forgotten/Charo" 184, 185
"Robber Bridegroom, The" 183-184
Robson, Mark 52, 58, 62
Rogers, Roy 9
Ross, Merrie Lynn 62, 64, 69, 74
Roundtree, Richard 52, 56
Rurgoff, Donald 26

Index

Salkowitz, Sy 170
Saltman, Shelly 102
Sargent, Joseph 35, 40-41, 63
Savalas, Telly 35, 36, **38**, 39, 186
"Save All My Brothers (Love Theme from Marjoe)" 208
Schlatter, George 181
"Secret Admirer, The" 192
Shankar, Ravi 14
Shatner, William 41, 42, **42**, 45, 186, 189
Shore, Sig 147, 150-151
Sidewinder 1 103-106, **105**, 223
Silk, Larry 26
Simon, Melvin 114
Ski Fascination 160
"Slay Ride" 189-191
Small, Mews 171-172
Smith, Howard 19, 25, 26, 28, 29, 30
Smith, Paul L. 131, 132, 135
Smith, Rex 204, 205
Snow, Hank 169
Speak Up, America 159, 186-187, 221
Spelling, Aaron 192, 194
Spielberg, Steven 40, 41
Spinell, Joe 117, 118, 121, 123
Stallone, Sylvester 66, 75, 156
Star Wars 90, 102, 117-118, 120, 178
Starcrash 117-124, **119**, **122**, 145, 219, 223
Steinberger, Charly 161
Street Hawk 204-205, 223
Struzan, Drew 90, **91**
Sundstrom, Cedric 151, 155, 156-158
Survivalist, The 147-151

T. J. Hooker 189-192, 223
Tanenbaum, Robert 106

Taylor, Roderick 201, 202
"Those City Lights" 72
Tosi, Mario 40
Toth 27, 28
Tubb, Ernest 169
"Turkish Connection, The" 180
Turley, Jack 41, 46
Twilight Tidings 7-8, 207

Van Rellin, Maxwell 16-17
Village of the Giants 86, 90
"Village of the Motorpigs" 201-203
Viva Knievel! 96-103, **97**, **100**, 216, 219, 223
Vogel, Virgil W. 201, 204
Von Theumer, Ernst R. 131, 135

Wambaugh, Joseph 169
"War Games" 169, 172-175
Werner, Wallace "Buddy" 160
West, Essie Binkley 5
West, Virginia 5, 6
"When a Man Loves a Woman" 197
When You Comin' Back, Red Ryder xi-xii, xiii, xv, 79, 106-117, **107**, **109**, **112**, **115**, 157, 169, 185, 215, 220, 221, 223, **224**, 227, 229, **231**
"Where Are You Hiding?" 178
Whiz Kids 195-198, 210, 224
Wild Bill 162-165, 223
Williams, Earle E. 207
Williams, Robin 135, 181-182
"Wind Up" 178
Wolfe, Louis P. 4-5
Wonder Woman 67, 75, 77
World's Youngest Evangelist 207
Woronov, Mary 136, 137, 139, 140, **141**, 142, 143

www.ingramcontent.com/pod-product-compliance
Lightning Source LLC
Chambersburg PA
CBHW062015220426
43662CB00010B/1338